Walking
AUSTRIA'S
ALPS
HUT TO HUT

by Jonathan Hurdle

With contributions by

George Mills
Bob Poore and Margaret Stickland
Belinda Swift
Jeremy Wilcox

The Mountaineers/Seattle

To Sara

*and to Ian, Adrian, Sandra,
Richard, and Anthony*

THE MOUNTAINEERS: Organized 1906
"...to explore, study, preserve, and enjoy the
natural beauty of the Northwest."

© 1988 by Jonathan Hurdle

Published by The Mountaineers
306 2nd Avenue West, Seattle, Washington 98119

Published simultaneously:
  in Canada by
    Douglas & McIntyre, Ltd.,
    1615 Venables Street, Vancouver, British Columbia V5L 2H1
  in Great Britain by
    Cordee, 3a DeMontfort Street
    Leicester, England LE1 7HD

Manufactured in the United States of America

Copy edited by Miriam Bulmer
Cover design by Elizabeth Watson
Layout by Nick Gregoric
Maps by Nick Gregoric
Cover photo: Berliner Hütte (Tour 6). Cecil Davies photo

Library of Congress Cataloging in Publication Data

Hurdle, Jonathan, 1957-
    Walking Austria's Alps.

    Includes index.
      1. Hiking — Austria — Alps, Austrian — Guide-books.
2. Walking — Austria — Alps, Austrian — guide-books.
3. Alps, Austrian (Austria) — Description and travel —
Guide-books.   I. Title.
GV199.44.A92A444   1988   914.36   88-1767
ISBN 0-89886-159-4 (pbk.)

Contents

Lindauer Hütte, Rätikon / Silvretta area (Cecil Davies photo)

Preface

This book tells you how to see some of the best mountain scenery in the world — up close. It will take you through valleys, over passes, and among Alpine peaks whose scale is heroic and whose beauty you only dreamed about. On these tours, the walker earns the satisfaction of seeing breathtaking mountain vistas that will be forever denied to those who restrict themselves to mechanized means of transport. Some of the walks here are classics, others are less well known, but all offer a full taste of the riches of the Alps.

Included here are details of walking tours in ten areas of the Austrian Alps. The tours are between four and eleven days in length and stop each night at one of Austria's mountain huts, where walkers can eat well and sleep in communal comfort. The huts, which allow the walker to travel unencumbered by camping equipment, are connected by a mountain footpath network that is well trodden and well marked but also provides plenty of challenges for adventurous walkers.

The daily itineraries presented here allow ample time for walkers to reach their destination so they can detour, climb nearby peaks, or simply stop to admire the spectacular scenery.

Embarking on one of these walks does not entail a commitment to spending days in the wilderness. Most of the tours are easily accessible to towns, villages, and roads, allowing walkers to choose just part of a route. No technical climbing skills or equipment are necessary for these tours, some of which go past glaciers and over peaks of more than 3000 meters where walkers may encounter snow patches. Two of the tours include short stretches actually over glaciers, but these are both, given good weather, quite safe for strong, surefooted, and experienced walkers.

Introduction

The pleasures of mountain walking are sometimes tainted by the heavy load of camping gear the walker has to carry in order to spend time in remote and beautiful areas. Not so in Austria, whose extensive system of mountain huts allows walkers who have no desire to camp out or carry a heavy pack to spend entire summers wandering easily through some of the world's finest mountain scenery. The huts offer good, hearty food and communal accommodations, letting walkers travel unencumbered by tents, cooking pots and the like.

The huts are linked by trails that are well marked and well trodden and take walkers through valleys, up mountainsides and over high passes, among the most spectacular mountain scenery. The trails visit small towns and mountain villages, but mostly they stay away from "civilization," allowing the walker to spend weeks wandering hut-to-hut in the high country.

The tours in this book are for strong walkers who have explored mountains and moorlands but who are not interested in breaking endurance records or their necks. They are for people who expect their mountain excursions to be energetic, but who also want plenty of time for dawdling, eating lunch, searching for edelweiss (don't pick them; it's illegal), or just admiring the view. Even so, the routes described here are not short on challenges. Altitudes are much higher than in the mountains of Britain or the eastern United States (much of your time will be spent over 2000 meters/6400 feet), and everything is on a much grander scale. Ascents of 1000 meters (3200 feet) are common. While no technical climbing skills are required, walkers should be prepared for steep gradients and much longer ascents than are found on any British mountain. Readers used to the mountains of western North America, however, will find comparable challenges in the Austrian Alps.

Most of the paths followed by these routes lead across open mountainsides, often over rocky surfaces and sometimes on scree. Some paths also cross grasslands. Glaciers are avoided wherever possible, but in a few cases it is necessary to cross them for short stretches. In good weather, these crossings require neither specialized equipment nor expertise and are quite safe for ordinary walkers. (The one exception to this is in the Ötztaler Alps; for details, see Tour 4.) Overall, the most demanding sections along the routes described in this book are short scrambles, sometimes requiring the use of hands, over ground too steep to support a proper path. These stretches are often aided by fixed cables, ropes, or steel rungs set into the rock and will be but a very small part of a day's route. Even so, they can be dangerous for inexperienced or incautious individuals.

Trail sign warns unwary hikers to beware of falling rocks. (Bob & Ira Spring photo)

Several types of aerial lifts provide easy access to Austria's mountain trails. (Tyrolean National Tourist Office, Innsbruck, photo)

Because the walks require no technical climbing, the principal qualifications for enjoying them are physical fitness, stamina, and a recognition that climbing 1000 meters with no major break in gradient is not an easy task. Many of the tours in this book contain sections in which walking is taken to its limits. While roped ascents are not included, the routes often cross precipitous terrain that demands "a head for the heights."

I have avoided assigning formal route grades because each day's walk is likely to span a wide range of difficulty. However, the introductions both to chapters and to individual days indicate the degree of difficulty to be expected.

Despite the above cautions, beginners need not be deterred. Provided that they are properly equipped, reasonably fit, and accompanied by experienced mountain walkers, they will be able to tackle and enjoy most of these walks. The terrain may be steep and rocky, but the distances between huts are generally short, making overnight trips feasible even for children, providing they are decently shod and have had a little practice in mountain walking. In fact, one of the nicest things about walking in the Austrian Alps is that you frequently meet entire Austrian or German families, including grandparents, who are out on day hikes or even multi-day hutting trips.

The Austrian Alps are not a wilderness. In fact, they are so well trodden that safety is not the problem it might be in remote areas of, say, Scotland or Alaska. In the Alps, however, the nearness of civilization, in the form of mountain villages and alpine huts, allows ordinary walkers to enjoy their glories without great hardship or danger.

AUSTRIA'S MOUNTAIN HUTS

About half of Austria's huts are owned and run by the German and Austrian alpine clubs. A membership in the UK branch of the Austrian Club is good for both and will get you a 50-percent reduction on accommodation charges in most huts. You can use the huts without a membership but on most trips, the fee will quickly pay for itself. Advance booking, which is advisable for groups (and only possible for club members), is arranged by contacting the hut warden at his valley address before the opening of the hut season or at the hut itself during the season. Addresses, phone numbers, hut opening times, and much other information is contained in *Die Alpenvereinshütten,* known in English as the "Green Hut Book," published by the AAC.

Alpine huts are not mountain shacks but well-equipped, cheap hostels, comparable to the best British and American youth hostels. They are clean, comfortable, and professionally run, but differ from the typical youth hostel in that accommodations are communal. Most hut accommodation consists of *Matratzenlager,* literally a "mattress camp," where long mattresses provide sleeping space for perhaps twenty people at a time, with no segregation by sex or age. This may cause some raised eyebrows among prudish visitors, but it is the most efficient way of accommodating large numbers of people in a small space. A few individual beds are available at higher prices.

Hut food is hearty and filling. For the main evening meal, you will usually find a choice of dishes except in the smallest huts, where you may have to be content with what's in the pot. The basic item of hut fare is *Bergsteigeressen,* "mountain climber's food," which is appropriately hot and hearty and probably will be the best value on the menu. Huts usually change their *Bergsteigeressen* every day, but the dish always contains some type of meat served with pasta, dumplings, potatoes, or some other form of filler. Other typical dishes include *Gulaschsuppe,* a spicy, thick stewlike soup

Hut visitors partake of kaiserschmarrn, a type of pancake often served in mountain huts. (Tyrolean National Tourist Office, Innsbruck, photo)

served with bread; *Leberkäse,* a slab of Spam-like meat sometimes served with an egg on top; *Knödel,* a big bready dumpling served with sauce, usually as an accompaniment to meat; *Tirolergröstl,* a hash of fried potatoes and meat; *Erbsensuppe,* pea soup; and *Frühlingsuppe,* vegetable soup.

Desserts are less numerous and some huts don't bother with them, but one of the best is *Kaiserschmarrn,* a vast pile of sugar-covered pancake pieces, served with a side dish of stewed fruit or jam. The pancakes tend to be very eggy, and this, together with the enormous size of the helpings, may explain why it is sometimes served as a main course. Huts also serve lunch and may sell you food to take on the road.

Other aspects of hut catering are less satisfactory. Tea and coffee are very expensive compared to the reasonable prices of main meals. The cost can be alleviated somewhat by taking your own, which means having to buy hot water — *Teewasser* — at maybe half the price of the beverage. Breakfast also tends to be overpriced, and rather dull, consisting of three or four slices of bread with prepacked butter, jam, and cheese. You may wish to stock up your own ingredients when visiting towns, as many of the locals do. Eggs are occasionally provided for breakfast, but never cereal. (I once caused great amusement by producing my own muesli (granola) at breakfast; the locals had never seen anything like it, despite muesli's carefully marketed image as a natural food from the Alps.) The basic hut food to be wary of, and another reason for avoiding breakfast, is the bread, which is hard, dry, and rather bitter.

Lager beer is available at the huts. It varies in quality, although almost any cold drink tastes good after a hard day's walk. Many huts also serve wines and spirits, such as the famous *Schnapps*.

The huts' washing facilities are usually basic, although always clean. Hot water in the washrooms is unusual and hot showers are a rarity. The difficulty of supplying both power and water to the huts — many have their own generators — explains this one note of primitivism.

LANGUAGE

Getting what you want in the huts will be a lot easier if you know a little German, although quite a few of the wardens speak some

English. So do a fair number of other walkers, but it is very useful to be able to ask them such things as how long it will take to get to the next hut without having to resort to English. Even if you speak no German you will still be able to make yourself understood, but you will find yourself left out of the hut social life, which can rise to quite a pitch on the nights when everybody starts to sing. A mountain hut in full cry is a sight to behold and gives the visitor a glimpse into Austrian culture surely not seen by tourists who confine themselves to cities.

WHEN TO GO

The huts are generally open from early July until mid-September — the Alpine summer season. The weather during this period is usually dry, clear and warm (often in the 70s), with little or no snow left on the paths from the previous winter. However, Alpine weather is notoriously fickle, and walkers should be prepared for rapid changes in wind, temperature, and precipitation. In the summer of 1985, two days of continual rain left the valleys of the Tyrol flooded and the mountain passes feet deep in snow; only a few hours before this deluge began, I was sitting in 80-degree sunshine, scoffing at reports that a major snowstorm was on its way.

HOW TO GET THERE

Innsbruck is the center of the region that contains most of the walks in this book. Direct flights are available from Britain and the U.S., but it will probably be cheaper and easier to fly either to Munich or Zürich, both of which have good train services to Innsbruck. These centers are actually better situated than Innsbruck for certain walks. The Rätikon/Silvretta route, for example, starts from Bludenz, west of Innsbruck and on the main train line from Zürich. Similarly, Munich offers better access than Innsbruck to the Karwendel. If you are aiming for the Glockner, Hafner, Ankogel regions or the Dachstein, then Zell-am-See or Lienz are centers of communication.

An independent touring package is offered by the Austrian Alpine Club and Ramblers Holidays. The seven- or fourteen-night package includes return air fare from London Gatwick to Innsbruck and in 1987 cost $265 (£177) for fourteen nights at current rates.

Austria has an excellent road network, with the main highways running in the valleys. Main highways link Austria with Germany to the north, Switzerland to the west, and Italy, via the Alpine tunnels, to the south. The smaller roads, too, are well maintained and offer generally good (although sometimes steep and winding) access deep into mountain areas. Leaving a car parked for a few days while walking a route should not be a problem, but walkers are advised to check with local tourist authorities before doing so.

TRAILS

Most of the trails on these tours are so well marked and well trodden that map and compass navigation is seldom necessary. Still, trails and their markings can easily disappear in snow, mist, or rain and so you should, as with any trip into the mountains, carry appropriate maps and a compass and know how to use them.

Trails are marked with red paint splashes on rocks, trees, and other wayside features. In some cases the painters' enthusiasm has got the better of them and they have left their mark every few yards.

Many paths also have other color codings, numbers, and sometimes names. Some or all of this information is presented on signposts and maps, with the result that it is quite difficult to get lost providing conditions are kind and you stay alert. A trail sign will also typically indicate the time in hours to its destination. "Hours" in German is *Stunden,* abbreviated as *Std.*

A standard warning on signposts is *nur für Geubte,* which means "only for the experienced." These signs are put up by local mountain clubs as a warning that the section you are about to enter is harder going. It will almost certainly involve a steep climb or descent or perhaps a difficult, loose, or rocky surface. The route may also include cables, rungs, or ropes fixed to the rock, and may well be accompanied by a precipitous drop. Whatever the specifics, no technical climbing will be required and the trail is still accessible to less experienced walkers provided they are accompanied by someone with experience of those conditions.

FLORA AND FAUNA

Probably the most familiar animal of the Alps is the marmot, a furry burrow-dweller about the size of a large domestic cat. They can be seen running about grassy mountainsides, but will be more often heard than seen, as they make a loud squeaking call. More spectacular but less common is the mountain deer known in French as *chamois* and in German as *Gimse*. They are likely to be seen in small herds clambering with great agility over impossibly steep and treacherous terrain.

Bird life is not generally abundant but there are pockets of avian activity. Common birds include the Alpine chough, an all-black bird distinguished by its short yellow bill. They are usually seen in noisy flocks wheeling around peaks, passes, and other high places. Look for Alpine accentors hopping about on grassy hill-

Chamois display great agility in rough terrain. (Bob & Ira Spring photo)

Alpine flowers, such as edelweiss, provide spots of brightness. (Bob & Ira Spring photo)

sides; in woods and scrubland the black redstart is not uncommon. You may also see dippers feeding in a fast-flowing stream or flying straight and low over the water. The golden eagle, known in German as *Steinadler,* is most likely to be seen soaring in thermals among the mountaintops.

Roughly half of Austria is forested, with the most extensive stands found in the foothills. At higher elevations, however, the overall impression is rather one of openness, with forests forming dark green accents in a landscape dominated by the lighter, brighter emerald of Alpine meadows. Below 500 meters elevation the forests are dominated by hardwoods, mainly beech, ash, sycamore, and oak. Between 500 and 1100 meters, the hardwoods are joined by conifers, especially larch, silver fir, and Scotch pine. These evergreens occur upslope to near timberline, where stunted, wind-twisted Arolla pines, mountain pines, and larches predominate. Some of the better-known Alpine flowers include gentian, Alpine pansy, primula, globe flower, silver thistle, soldanella, Alpine poppy, and, of course, the famous Alpine edelweiss.

GENERAL EQUIPMENT

The existence of Austria's mountain huts allows walkers to take much less gear, since they need not carry tents and cooking equipment. Consequently, the bulk of the equipment taken by a walker on these tours will be clothing. Mountain weather should never be underestimated, so sufficient warm and waterproof clothing should be taken to cope with wind, rain, and snow. Be sure to take a complete change of clothes in case of a soaking; they will be worth every ounce in your pack. Take as many socks and T-shirts as you reasonably can carry; your exertions will ensure a high turnover of these. Hopefully, the weather will allow you to walk in shorts, but if not you will be glad of woolen breeches, especially at higher altitudes.

Everything should be packed in a serviceable backpack, which should be lined with a large plastic bag such as a garbage bag. (I have yet to see a truly waterproof backpack, despite appearances to the contrary.) In general, take the absolute minimum of gear, for you will regret every unnecessary ounce on your way up the first pass. You are on vacation, but if you treat your equipment list as an exercise in asceticism, your vacation will be the better for it — as will your back. I have known minimalist travelers to take a small amount of toothpaste in a plastic bag rather than in its heavier tube; to discard pages of a novel as they are read; and even to jettison a whole book halfway up the first major climb of a walking trip.

More specialized clothing should include gaiters for rain, snow, mud, or long grass; a sunhat; a woolen hat; and sunglasses.

Perhaps the most important single item is a water bottle. This should hold at least two pints and have a secure but easily removable screw top. Your body loses a great deal of water in climbing, even in cool weather, and you will need constant replenishment. You will often cross mountain streams, which I have always found safe to drink from, but you may not wish to rely on them.

Leave your camping gear at home. Since the huts are so plentiful and well-equipped, tents are not needed. A sleeping bag is also unnecessary, as blankets are provided in the huts. A sheet sleeping bag or similar liner to separate sleeper from blankets is a good idea but is not required by hut management.

Whether you take ropes, crampons, and an ice axe depends on the area you choose to walk in, the route options you take when you get there, and the experience of your party. In normal summer conditions, all but two of the routes here do not require any of these items, and carrying them will only make your pack heavier than necessary. However, if there is a sudden snowfall; if there has been a cold spring, delaying the thaw of winter snow and ice; or especially if you wish to make extended trips on glaciers, then this gear will be at least very useful, if not indispensable. But you must know how to use them to begin with. Within this book, however, there are two routes for which an ice axe, at least, is strongly recommended: Tour 4, the Ötztaler Alps from Obergurgl to Vent, and Tour 6, the Zillertal High Route. For more detailed advice on equipment see those chapters.

BOOTS

The most important single factor determining the success of a walking trip is the condition of your feet. Blisters or other foot problems can quickly ruin an otherwise successful trip. Many walking tours have turned into painful endurance tests for those whose boots are not worn in, are ill-fitting, or are inadequate. Consider the amount of work your feet are going to do and protect them accordingly.

Your boots should have thick Vibram or other nonslip soles with a good tread, and high sides to provide ankle support for the rough and rocky surfaces over which you will be traveling.

Make sure the boots are entirely comfortable before you go by simulating walking conditions as far as possible: climb a steep hill with some weight on your back to see whether your heels survive being forced repeatedly against the back of the boot. Allow for a breaking-in period if you plan to purchase boots for these walks. Emphatically, *do not* wear new boots unless you are absolutely sure they are not going to create blisters. It is better to wear an old pair that might not be quite so waterproof or look quite so good, simply because you know they will not tear your feet to ribbons.

Modern variations on the traditional leather boot include lightweight boots and double-layer plastic boots, but these may be too hot and heavy for summer walking.

Despite the best preparation, it is a rare walker whose feet emerge completely unscathed from a walking tour. Therefore, be sure to take plenty of adhesive dressings, moleskins, and antiseptic cream.

Many excellent maps of Austria's mountains are available. (Tyrolean National Tourist Office, Innsbruck, photo)

MAPS

The great popularity of the Austrian Alps is shown by the profusion of maps for the whole region, many designed specifically for walkers. The most detailed is the 1:25,000 series produced by the Alpine Club; you can get them at a discount with membership. Unfortunately, these maps do not cover every Alpine area.

I find the 1:50,000 Kompass Wanderkarte maps perfectly good and, while not as detailed as the larger scale maps, they are more economical because you have to buy fewer of them. The back of each map contains much information on the area it covers including towns, valleys, footpaths, and huts. Freytag and Berndt publishes 1:50,000 and 1:100,000 series, although the latter is too small for detailed navigation.

Protect your maps with a clear plastic map case. This is an important piece of equipment, as without it maps will quickly become damaged and illegible. The Kompass maps are available from Stanfords of Long Acre, London WC2, or from the English branch of the Austrian Alpine Club. When buying Alpine maps, be aware that some are published specifically for skiers and consequently will not feature walking trails.

EMERGENCY SUPPLIES

You should carry a first-aid kit containing a sun block, ointment for burns and insect bites, elastic bandage for strapping up twisted ankles, yards and yards of adhesive dressings, and antiseptic cream for dressing blisters.

On these tours you will never be more than three or four hours from a hut or village, but you should also pack an emergency supply of high-energy foods such as glucose tablets or dried fruit, in case you get stranded due to weather or injury.

If you become lost or somehow immobilized on a mountainside in darkness or clouds, keeping warm is the top priority. Carry a large plastic survival bag or foil blanket. If you get lost or lose touch with your party, a flashlight and/or whistle can let others know where you are. The standard European distress signal is six blasts on a whistle, six shouts, or six repetitions of anything, followed by a minute's silence, repeat then six more whistles, and so on.

The recommended minimum party size for any mountain walking trip is three people, so that if one gets injured, another can stay with the injured while the third goes for help. A larger group can be more fun but rather unwieldy, as people inevitably get strung out due to different walking speeds. In theory, a group should go at the speed of its slowest member, but this tends not to happen, so I suggest keeping your group size small.

THE AUSTRIAN ALPINE CLUB

The Austrians' love of their mountains and their recognition of the need to preserve them for everyone to enjoy resulted in the formation of the Österreichische Alpenverein (OAV) in Vienna in 1862. Its aim was to promote visits to the Alps by offering cheap transportation and accommodation for members. It was also hoped that some scientific work would be done but this justification soon became secondary to the pure enjoyment of the mountains. The United Kingdom branch, the Austrian Alpine Club (AAC), was founded in 1948. It now has about 4000 members.

The OAV, together with its West German equivalent, the Deutscher Alpenverein (DAV), and the South Tyrol Alpine Club (AVS) in Italy, owns 553 huts in and on the borders of Austria. Another 558 huts listed by the "Green Hut Book" are run by smaller clubs or are privately owned.

Apart from access to huts, advantages offered to members include: group liability insurance against third-party claims; a special deal for personal insurance with an English insurance company; a rail card entitling holders to 25 percent off the price of a round-trip journey over 140 kilometers on Austrian state railways; reciprocal agreements with hutting organizations in other European countries; a quarterly newsletter; and walkers' maps.

The categories of membership (with 1987 fees in both dollars and pounds) are as follows: adult $22.50/£15; spouse $16.50/£11; and family (parents plus two children under 18 years of age) $36/£24. An extra $1/£.75 provides members with a *Hüttenmark,* a special stamp giving access to huts run by a number of clubs other than the OAV or DAV. Overseas applicants are asked to pay by bank drafts made out in pounds sterling. The address of the British Branch of the AAC is 13 Longcroft House, Fretherne Road, Welwyn Garden City, Herts., England AL8 6PQ; telephone (0707) 324835.

Americans can join the Österreichische Alpenverein through the Austrian National Tourist Office, 500 5th Avenue, New York, NY 10110; telephone (212) 944-6880. Applicants should be sure to allow two months for processing.

ACCESS

The *Access* note at the beginning of each day's narrative indicates the nearest road or village. You will never be more than a couple of hours' walk from civilization, whether it be a hut, a road, or a town. Even if a particular day's walk has no direct access points, you should be able to reach it without much difficulty due to the large number of footpaths in the area.

SAFETY CONSIDERATIONS

The fact that a trip or area is described in this book is not a representation that it is a safe one for your group. This book does not list every hazard that may confront you — and can't, due to changing terrain and weather, and the varying capabilities of different travelers. You assume responsibility for your own safety when you travel, and must exercise your own independent judgment. Political considerations may add to the risks of travel in Europe in ways that this book cannot predict. When you travel you assume this risk, and should keep informed of political developments that may make safe travel difficult or impossible.

The Mountaineers

⚮ TOUR 1 ⚮

The Lechtaler Alps

Route: *Bödele – Freschen Haus – Faschina –*
Biberacher Hütte – Göppinger Hütte – Ravensburger Hütte –
Ülmer Hütte – Ansbacher Hütte – Memminger Hütte –
Steinsee Hütte – Anhalter Hütte – Nassereith

This walk of about 160 kilometers (100 miles) through the western end of the Austrian Alps stretches from Bödele near Bregenz to Nassereith near Imst, spending much of its distance in the Lechtaler Alps above the Inn Valley. It is divided here into stages of less than 16 kilometers a day for a tour of a little under two weeks, and is within the capabilities of anyone with a little walking experience who wants to explore some spectacular mountain country — and have time to stop and look at it.

The route forms the Alpine section of the trans-European footpath E4, which runs between the Pyrenees, the Jura, and the Neusiedlersee in eastern Austria. This section of the E4 is called the *Weitwanderweg* 01 ("Long-distance Footpath 1") in Austria and the route described here is part of it. Being a principal footpath, it is generally well signposted and well trodden, although some sections are physically and navigationally more demanding than others. The path is marked throughout by 201 and 601 signs, indicating different parts of the Weitwanderweg.

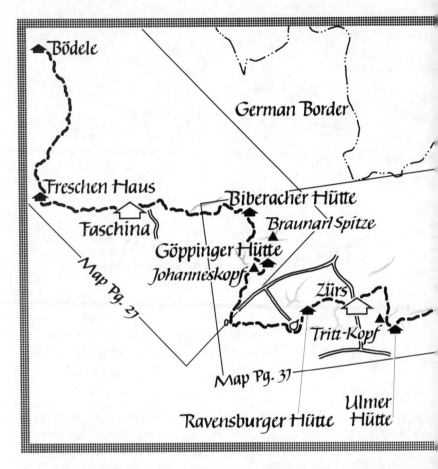

The maximum altitude is about 2700 meters (8850 feet) and much of the route is above 2000 meters (6560 feet). From late June until early October walkers should have to cope with only a few isolated patches of snow, removing the need for ice axes, crampons, or rope. This is a walk rather than a climbing expedition, but some sections are very steep and a few stretches become scrambles. These parts are said to be the most difficult of the entire Weitwanderweg, but even for beginners — providing they are properly equipped, competently led, and reasonably fit — they should hold no terrors.

Access to this route is limited because it passes through few towns or villages, but you are never far from civilization. The Inn Valley, with its excellent visitor facilities, is the most obvious place

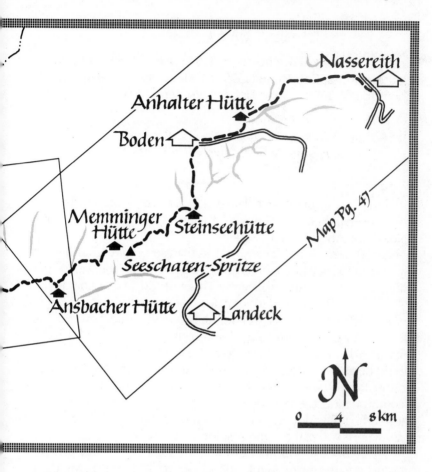

to begin. You can get to Bödele, at the beginning of the route, via bus service from Dornbirn (south of Bregenz), while Nassereith is served by buses to Imst, Innsbruck, and the Inn Valley.

Maps: Kompass Wanderkarte 1:50,000 series: No. 2, Bregenzerwald – Westgallen; No. 32, Bludenz-Shruns – Klostertal; No. 33, Arlberg – Nordl – Verwallgruppe; No. 34, Landeck – Nordl – Samnaungruppe; and No. 35, Imst – Telfs – Kuhtai. Also available are the Freytag and Berndt 1:100,000 Wanderkarten, of which you need sheet 36, Bregenzerwald, and sheet 35, Lechtaler und Allgauer Alpen. These are appealing for the sake of economy, but I find they are on too small a scale for detailed navigation. The western section of this route is not, at time of writing, covered by the Alpenverein 1:25,000 series.

DAY 1

Bödele (1140 m) to Freschen Haus (1846 m) via Lustenauer Hütte (1250 m), Weissefluh Hütte (1375 m), Mörzelspitze (1830 m), Altenhof Alpe (c. 1750 m) and Hoher Freschen (2004 m)

Time: 7 hours
Distance: 19 kilometers (11.78 miles)
Viewpoints: Mörzelspitze; Hoher Freschen
Access: Bödele

This long and difficult first day's walk may be broken in two by staying overnight at the Weissefluh Hütte. The walk contains one major climb: the Hoher Freschen.

If you start from Bödele with less than seven or eight hours of daylight ahead of you, it would be as well to head for the Weissefluh Hütte, about two hours' walk away. This will add an extra day to the walk, and could create problems for those intending to walk the whole route in two weeks. Weissefluh Hütte is privately owned, but you can still get in with your Alpenverein card, provided it has a Hüttenmarke. If you are starting from Bödele early in the day you should be able to complete the route. Alternatively, you could aim for the farmhouse at Altenhof Alpe, but this is not a hut and accommodation there is only by grace and favor of the farmer. There is no hut at Bödele, but you should be able to find at least one hotel where you can eat and rest for a reasonable price.

From Bödele, follow the road east for a short way and go through a gate on the right side of the road. The first signpost presents itself at the gate, directing walkers to the Lustenauer Hütte, one hour away. You will pass a 201 sign on a tree on your left. The track to the Lustenauer presents neither navigational problems nor steep gradients. It winds through pleasant pine woods, used mostly for forestry, and has views to the east.

From the Lustenauer, the terrain continues much the same for about 2 kilometers but gets wetter underfoot in the vicinity of the Bregenzer Hütte. The track is well marked. You emerge from the woods south of the Bregenzer Hütte and make your first real climb to the farm hut at Weissefluh.

The track down from Weissefluh is car-sized and leads to a wooded valley where you will find a road leading to the farm of Untersehren Alpe, overshadowed by the Mörzelspitze, harbinger

Starting the walk at Bodele. Note distinctive trail marker on tree. (Ian Anderson photo)

of more serious walking. Turn right at the farm and make your way up the grassy slopes towards Obersehrenalpe. The path gets steeper and muddier but is well trodden and well marked. It comes to a grassy prominence above the Obersehrenalpe farm building and with a spectacular and not altogether undaunting view of the path leading up the side of the Mörzelspitze ridge. Above you and in the direction of that path is a sign you should head for and then follow.

This signpost is not of great strategic significance, but it is a first for walkers of this route. The way, it says, is *nur für Geübte,* which serves as both a warning and a tribute. The *Geübte* (pronounced "ge-oobta") are the initiates, the wise and wiry mountain folk whose experience in these places allows them to travel where ordinary people may not. The signs are put up by local mountain clubs to indicate the difficulty of the route ahead. "Only for the initiates" says you should be prepared for tough gradients, rough conditions underfoot, and perhaps precipitous drops by the side of your path. Despite the dire warnings you can walk a little taller after passing this sign because you are now, either by justification or self-appointment, one of the *Geubte*.

Red and yellow signs guide you to the top of this first climb, where, weather permitting, a wonderful view to the east will unfold as your line of vision tops the narrow ridge. You may share the experience of nineteenth-century mountaineer Sir Claude Schuster, who spoke of "the moment of ecstasy when your head reaches the level of the arete and all the glorious spires and domes, ramparts and battlements leap into view at once. You gasp at them, partly from admiration and partly from lack of breath...."

When you get your breath back, turn right at the ridge, climb a little further, and follow the peaks marked by red and yellow signs. The path starts to descend to the left after the Mörzelspitze summit and you should continue along the ridge and down a steep track through a patch of trees and small bushes, with the farm buildings of the Oberbrudertannalpe below and to your left.

Next, descend to a saddle between the Mörzelspitze and the Salzböden Kopf, at which point the path forks. The sign for the right fork points to Unterfluh Alpe, but you must take the left, which leads, indistinctly at first, uphill in a southwesterly direction to skirt around the east side of the Salzböden summit. When you get to the top you can see the dramatic cliff below and to your right that marks the abrupt termination of the gently sloping high pasture of Altenhof Alpe.

The farm on the south side of this pasture may provide you with shelter for the night if the light is fading or your energy is flagging. From here it is a tough two-and-a-half-hour walk over the Hoher Freschen and down the other side to the Freschen Haus. This section contains possibly the most dangerous stretch of the entire route and should not be attempted if the light or the weather is bad or if you are tired. If you do decide to stop the night at Altenhof, the locals there will probably tell you it was the best thing you could have done.

Altenhof is not an inn or hut and the farmer is not obliged to offer accommodation. If he does, you will find yourself in a dark wooden building that exists for cattle as much as it does for humans: a sizeable part of the ground floor is actually a cow shed. The building has no electricity and its water supply is a nearby

1
▲ Bödele 1148

201 ▲ Lustenauer Hütte 1250

Höhe
Freschen
2004
▲

▲ Morzelspitle
▲ Altenhof Alpe 1830

2
▲ Freschen Haus 1846

▲ Göfiser Höhe

Damüls 1431

3
Faschina
▲ Zafernhorn 2107

601
Hochschere 2013
▲ Zitterklapfen 2403

4
Biberacher Hütte 1845 ◄

Johanneskopf 2507 ▲
Braunarl-Spitze
▲2649

Göppinger Hütte 2245

N

0   2   4 km

spring. You sleep in a hayloft upstairs. Nothing could be more enticing after a hard day's walk and it seems the very stuff of romance and adventure. But be warned: the loft is separated from the cows by nothing more than the clear mountain air, which is an excellent carrier of the sound of cowbells. The tinkle of cowbells can be a pleasant memory to take away from the Alps, but not if they torment you from dusk to dawn.

If you fancy a good night's sleep, and other factors are favorable, it's as well to press on to the Freschen Haus. The path from Altenhof splits at the northeast corner of the pasture, near a winding station for the cable car. Both tracks lead to the Hoher Freschen and join again after about 1 kilometer. The one on the left climbs fairly easily up a muddy track. After reuniting both tracks, the path, marked with red and white, runs over some grassy mountainside before starting the serious climb to the summit of the Hoher Freschen. This section is prefaced with another, more explicit notice saying this *really* is *nur für Geubte*. It begins with some steep scrambles up rocky and muddy slopes and continues with a short walk along a perilously thin ridge of rock with precipitous drops on both sides. Beyond the ridge, cables are set into the rock at various points to help you up. This section requires great care.

The Freschen Haus is no more than half an hour's walk from the top, which is marked by a metal sign. It is a large modern hut, recently rebuilt, as the plaques outside and the photographs inside will testify. If you have made it from Bödele in a day, you will be especially glad of its comforts.

DAY 2

Freschen Haus (1846 m) to Faschina (c. 1440 m) via Göfiser Höhe (1788 m)

Time: 4 hours
Distance: 12 kilometers (7.44 miles)
Viewpoints: Freschen Haus
Access: Damüls

This is a gentle half-day walk at the most and may give you a chance to recuperate after yesterday's exertions. Damüls also provides a rare opportunity to buy food, change money, stock up on adhesive

Crossing on alpine meadow, the Hochschere in background. (Ian Anderson photo)

dressings and so on before going back into the mountains. The next town you come to will be Zürs — in four days' time.

Go through the Alpengarten above the Freschen Haus and head east along the side of the Höhe Matona. Soon you will come to the first indication that you are on the trans-European E4 footpath: the letters are painted on a rock by the side of the path.

The walk roughly follows the mountain's contours, passing a footpath junction just below the Göfiser Höhe. Take the left branch, which is signposted to Damüls. It is a fine mountainside walk from here to Alpe Portla, where a small road is visible near farm buildings. Stay off the road for as long as possible by following the mountain path a short way above it for about half a kilometer until the path leads down to join the road. It is a pleasant 2 kilometer walk from here to the small town of Damüls, although the paved road may be hard underfoot.

Damüls, the highest village in the Bregenzerwald, marks the point at which Fernwanderweg 201 becomes 601, the number it bears for the rest of the walk. The first 601 sign is on the wall of a shop and it points down the hill from the main street. After a short way, turn right onto a gravel road leading to a bridge over a river. Do not continue into the pine wood that lies in front of you as you walk away from the town.

This is a short day and should leave you time to explore Damüls, one of the few villages en route. It is a well-known skiing center in winter, and in summer is known for its picturesque qualities. It was allegedly founded by five Swiss families who fled over the mountains into free Austria. The people here are said to speak a dialect the Swiss can understand, but not their Austrian neighbors. Damüls is mostly known for its fifteenth-century Gothic church, the Maria Kirche, which stands out against the mountain scenery with its bulbous dome and octagonal tower. Inside the church is a well-preserved series of frescoes painted in 1500.

It is a steep and not very inspiring walk of about twenty minutes up the hill to Faschina, a village well stocked with hotels. Alternatively, accommodation can be found in Damüls.

DAY 3

Faschina (c. 1440 m) to Biberache Hütte (1845 m) via Hochschere (2013 m)

> *Time:* 6 hours
> *Distance:* 13 kilometers (8.06 miles)
> *Viewpoints:* Hochschere; south from the
> side of the Zitterklapfen
> *Access:* Faschina

This is a serious day's walk, rather more difficult than Day 1, although not quite as long. It contains the hardest climb of the whole route and some tricky mountainside traverses. The scenic rewards are appropriately marvelous.

Near the top of the hill, on the road back to Damüls, look out for signposts on the side of a farmhouse on your left. These mark the start of the Hochschereweg and give lots of dire warnings about the route being *nur für Geubte.* You will see what they mean. Blue and yellow color coding starts here and accompanies the signs the whole way up. Go through the farm, across a field, and then steeply up a muddy track in a roughly northeasterly direction. The track is roughly parallel to the Damüls – Au road, which is visible, weather permitting, far below for much of the initial ascent.

After about 2 kilometers, the path stops following the contours and climbs brutally across them towards the Zafern Horn. It zigzags tightly across pasture before turning into a magnificent sweep across the scree-ridden north side of the Zafern Horn. This stretch leads to a ridge pointing to the Hochschere and other places. Follow the Hochschere sign, but heed another one that says *nach 80 m links fahren,* "turn left after 80 meters." This is an approximate distance, but the important thing is to find a track that reestablishes your generally easterly direction and heads you towards the farm at Zafera Alpe.

It is a pleasant grassy walk gently down to the farm over a magnificent open mountainside, but with few red and white markers to guide you. You will probably hear marmots squeaking as they run around the mountainside.

The isolated farm of Zafera Alpe is a good place to gird your loins before starting your assault on the extraordinary Hochschere, although by the time you have climbed it you may have other adjectives in mind. Follow the 601 sign on the side of the farm building and walk along the mountainside beneath the Zitterklapfen and the Hochschere until you cross a stream about half a kilometer from the farm. Turn right directly after the stream and head steeply up the mountain, walking next to the stream. Looking up, you will see a huge, wall-like scree field topped with jagged rock. This is the Hochschere. It looks impossible, if not for climbers, then certainly for walkers. But there is a way up, albeit a relentlessly steep one, and it is well marked and well maintained.

At the bottom, the path leaves the line of the stream and starts the zigzag that will take you to the top. It is a surprisingly stable, well-engineered path in view of the fact that it is mostly over scree. Rocks are paint-marked frequently and the most difficult sections, near the top, are accompanied by steel cable held into the rock. The local climbing club made the path passable, and is honored — and so it should be — on a plaque set into the rock near the top. Allow one and a half hours for the climb.

The path east from the Hochschere and along the south side of the Zitterklapfen is initially steep and loose. After losing height quickly it makes its way more or less levelly along the mountainside. The surface is rough and rocky and you must cross trees and streams. The Diesner Höhe to the south watches your progress as you keep roughly the same height along the side of the Zitterklapfen. A muddy stretch passes a farm and then starts to rise towards the Pregimel Bach. Leaving the farm behind, the track runs spectacularly along the side of the Glattjöchl Spitze to a point where it rises sharply and crosses the Pregimel Bach.

Climb a short way and then emerge onto a saddle to see the farm building of Ober Ischkarnei Alpe. The path passes to the east of the farm and above it, but take care not to stray too far up the hill or you will have to spend extra time coming down again in order to find the track that is the final approach to the Biberache Hütte.

Take a sharp turn east through a gate a short way below the farm. The hut should be visible from here, directly up the valley to the east, twenty to thirty minutes away. The track leads steadily up the left-hand side of the valley.

DAY 4

Biberache Hütte (1845 m) to Göppinger Hütte (2245 m) via the Lutz Valley (1502 m)

> *Time:* 4 hours
> *Distance:* 10 kilometers (6.2 miles)
> *Viewpoints:* Northeast on the climb to the Göppinger
> *Access:* Road from Lech or the Grosse Walsertal

The Biberache Hütte marks the beginning of a southward turn in the route. Looking south from the terrace of the hut, you can see the range containing the Johannes Kopf, the Schwarze Wand, the Bratschen Kopf, and other peaks. The good news is that you will shortly be among them. The bad news is that to get there you must first descend more than 300 meters to the Lutz Valley and then climb more than 700 meters to the hut. This is a tough walk, but fittingly spectacular.

The 601 sign at the Biberache points south through a gate and over fields that slope gently downhill before descending steeply towards the Lutz River valley. It is quite a difficult descent, with the path narrow, stony, and covered with roots. It passes through an area of stunted coniferous trees before coming, near the bottom, to a narrow plank bridge over a rushing stream. A brief walk along the mountainside just above the river leads to another plank bridge that takes you to a small road serving the valley farms. Turn left at the road and walk along it for a short way. Turn off at a right-hand hairpin bend, and follow a sign for the Göppinger Hütte.

This is the beginning of a tough climb that will last at least two hours and is unrelentingly steep for most of it, although well

View from path, near Biberacher Hütte (Ian Anderson photo)

marked and well trodden. There are good views of the Braunarl Spitze and Orgel Spitze on the way up.

The worst of the climb is over when you get to an extraordinary lake bed near the top. It is oasislike after the jagged rock of most of the climb. Walk blissfully over this soft grassy lake bed before resuming the final climb to the Göppinger. The climb is more gradual now, and very barren and rocky.

The hut, like many you yearn for at the end of a hard climb, appears sooner than you expect. The Göppinger is at the cross-roads of tracks coming from four directions and in the midst of some marvelous country. It is not far from Lech and close to the road connecting that village with the Freiburger Hütte. All this makes it very popular, so you should not be surprised, if you arrive late in the afternoon, to find yourself billeted in the Winterraum, a hidey-hole normally reserved for skiers but used as an overspill in summer. Like the rest of the hut, it gets very cozy on a fine summer weekend.

A night in the Göppinger may acquaint you with the finer points of Austrian/German mountain attire. As befits the serious-ness of Alpinism, mountain dress is a tightly regulated convention and non-Germanic travelers are often conspicuous by their maverick mountain gear. Knee breeches are perhaps the most ubiquitous item, and they are worn by everyone — young, old, male, female. They are usually made of green corduroy and fas-tened just below the knee by a small buttoned flap. Below the breeches and almost as *de rigueur* are long woolen socks, usually bright red and often decorated with embroidered patterns. Below these, and naturally the most important feature of the walker's attire, are the boots. With their huge Vibram soles and massive leather uppers coming up over the ankle, they make lesser boots look like slippers.

Other items of native mountain wear are more variable, but the men often wear loud red-and-white-checked shirts. Many also wear trilby-style felt hats; these may have a small feather in the band and quite often are adorned with badges and brooches. Some hats are pyramid shaped, and make the wearer look like a garden gnome.

The most sensible item of Germanic mountain gear is the small rucksack. Not everyone carries one, as many people travel in large groups, but those who do make the sack as small as possible. Carrying a large rucksack loaded with supposedly indispensable gear often invites derision. An old woman hobbling down a moun-tain carrying nothing but two sticks once asked me, as I was sweating upwards beneath a heavy pack, whether I was carrying my *Bettzimmer* (bedroom) with me. Your holiday will be much more enjoyable without all that extra weight.

DAY 5

Göppinger Hütte (2245 m) to Ravensburger Hütte (1947 m) via Freiburger Hütte (1918 m)

> *Time:* 7 hours
> *Distance:* 20 kilometers (12.4 miles)
> *Viewpoints:* The initial climb from the Göppinger.
> This is quite spectacular the whole way —
> the finest scenery so far. Also, eastwards
> from the Gehrengrat.
> *Access:* Freiburger Hütte

This long day's walk has some difficult conditions underfoot, but no severe climbs. The path to the Freiburger Hütte is well marked with red paint on the rocks the whole way. It is clearly signposted and leaves the Göppinger in a southwesterly direction, making its way over rocky ground and leaving to the right the path you came up yesterday. The path clings, sometimes a little tenuously, to the side of this crumbling valley that vegetation seems long ago to have forsaken. You will have to scramble over steep loose ground and perhaps patches of snow, so the going will be slow, especially if there are other parties of walkers on this understandably popular section. Something in this climb holds the essence of the high Alps: the harshness of the rock and snow; the stark contrast between the gray rock, white snow, and (hopefully) the sharp blue of the Alpine sky; the steady narrowing of the valley, bringing it all close and surrounding the senses.

The culmination of the climb — to a ridge of the Hirschen Spitze — is in every sense the high point of the morning's walk. You can survey the great sweep of the valley whose side you have just traversed: to the southwest is the Rote Wand and to the southeast the Spüllersee, your destination for the day.

The beginning of the descent towards the Freiburger is steep, loose, and rocky. At the bottom, cross a valley floor and go on to a very difficult stretch where the route is not so much a track as the best way through a mass of boulders. The only rule is to take the line of least resistance, keeping an eye out for the vital red marks. You may have to remove your pack at one stage in order to lower yourself, with the aid of a cable set into the rock, down a small rock face.

The path becomes less arduous as it winds round the side of the Rote Wand and the valley leading to the Freiburger comes into view. The road between the hut and Lech is visible in the valley and so is a small building at the point where the track meets the road. This is not, you may be disappointed to find, the Freiburger, which lies another twenty- to thirty-minute walk up the valley. A sign at the farm, when you get there, gives two alternative routes to the hut. One, via a car-size track around the side of the Formarin See, takes fifteen minutes longer than the other, which is the official 601 route. The latter, a well-trodden track high above the lake, will be very inviting if the sun is shining, but also, I am reliably informed, very cold. At this point you may be joined by quite a few other walkers, many of whom have left their cars at the farm at the head of the lake. This car access helps explain the size of the Freiburger hut, probably the least hutlike of any on this route.

Lunch at the Freiburger will fuel you for a tough afternoon's walk over the Gehrengrat to the Spüllersee and the Ravensburger Hütte just the other side of it. If you feel weighed down by lunch or lack energy, here is a rare opportunity to detour and rejoin the route near the end of the day while avoiding a major climb. The Spüllersee can be reached with little effort by retracing your steps to the other end of the Formarin See and then following the road toward Lech until a right turn takes you up the valley by the Spüller Bach to the lake itself. Walkers who hope to give their feet a rest should be warned that the roads are paved and can inflict a different kind of punishment on the feet than the path over the mountains.

I recommend that you not take the roads, because the way over the top is quite stunning in its higher reaches; it would be a shame to miss the views from the Gehrengrat.

To start the journey, follow the sign by the side of the Freiburger that points to the Ravensburger via 601, which leads up a rocky track and over farmland quite steeply. It is well marked with red paint. These red markers are useful guides over a stretch of limestone pavement broken by deep fissures. On the other side of this, walk across a pleasant green stretch below the Schafloch before starting the steep climb to the Gehrengrat, over 2400 meters.

Your climb zigzags not over crumbling rocky surfaces but over a grassy mountainside.

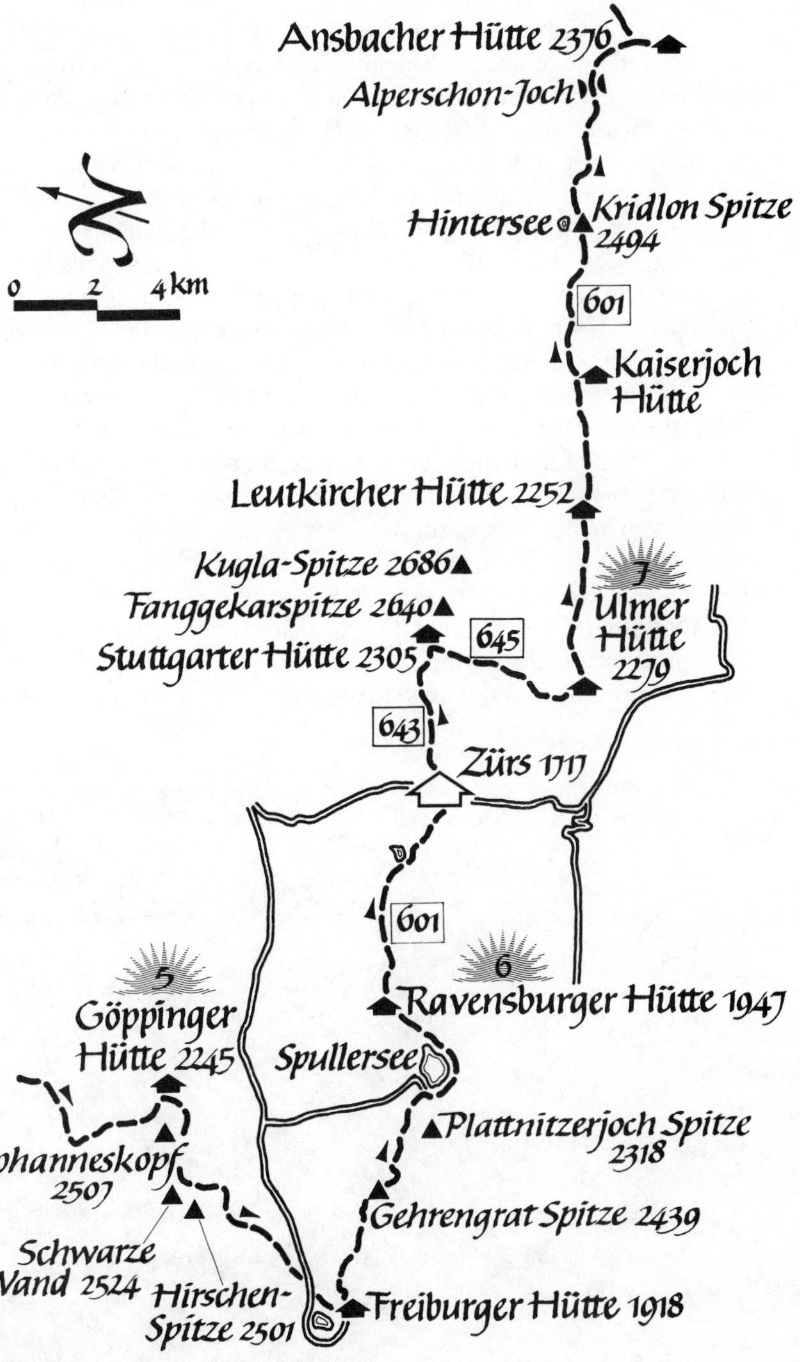

Ansbacher Hütte 2376

Alperschon-Joch

N

0   2   4 km

Hintersee ⊙ Kridlon Spitze
2494

601

Kaiserjoch
Hütte

Leutkircher Hütte 2252

Kugla-Spitze 2686▲

Fanggekarspitze 2640▲

Stuttgarter Hütte 2305

645

7

Ulmer
Hütte
2279

643

Zürs 1717

601

5

Göppinger
Hütte 2245

Spullersee

6

Ravensburger Hütte 1947

Johanneskopf
2507

▲Plattnitzerjoch Spitze
2318

Gehrengrat Spitze 2439

Schwarze
Wand 2524   Hirschen-
Spitze 2501

Freiburger Hütte 1918

From the Gehrengrat you look down on a glorious view of the Gamsboden Spitze and the Ganahis Kopf to the south. To the east, the Spüllersee appears vivid blue, surrounded by high peaks and marking the end of today's journey. If you are not in a hurry to get to the hut, it is worth lingering to savor the overall panorama: it will probably be one of the enduring images of your trip.

When you can pull yourself away, follow the ridge on which you stand eastwards until it plunges steeply to the left. Make your way gingerly down a steep, crumbling path with the Pfaffeneck looking down on you. Cross a stream and leave the Plattnitzer Jochspitze to your right as you descend towards the Spüllersee. When you reach the road that runs around the shore of the lake, follow the sign that directs you right to the Ravensburger Hütte via 601, rather than following your navigational instinct to turn left. The 601 road provides you with a pleasant run-in most of the way to the hut and you avoid contending with any more gradients, which the route to the north of the lake will entail and which by this stage of the day your legs may not appreciate.

Your circumnavigation of the lake takes you over a dam wall on the southern side, from which you should have a wonderful view of the snowcapped Silvretta range to the south. You are now above the

Late August snow between Goppinger and Freiburger Hüttes (Ian Anderson photo)

valley containing the Alfenz River, a tributary of the Inn River, whose valley runs parallel to your walk for the rest of the journey. At many places from now on, you will be able to look down into the Inn Valley and south to the Silvretta Alps.

The Ravensburger Hütte is a short distance up the hill from the lake. Like many of the other huts on the route, it is German-owned and named after the town its members come from. It is one of the most pleasant huts along the "01" and has managed to retain its traditional mountain hut feel by leaving the *Gaststube* unrenovated while thoroughly modernizing the rest of the hut. The kitchen is cafeteria style, with a one-way waiting line, stainless steel serving units, and a digital cash register. The sleeping accommodation is spotless and clad in immaculate new pine throughout.

DAY 6

Ravensburger Hütte (1947 m) to Ulmer Hütte (2279 m) via Zürser See (2150 m), Zürs (1717 m) and Stuttgarter Hütte (2305 m)

Time: 7 to 8 hours
Distance: 18 kilometers (11.16 miles)
Viewpoints: Approach to the Tritt Scharte from the north
Access: Zürs

This is not a difficult day's walk; there are few steep gradients and they are left to the end. The route passes through Zürs, a popular ski area, so use the opportunity to visit the shops, banks, and post office.

Zürs exists almost entirely for skiers and so is effectively a ghost town for summer walkers, with most of the buildings bearing signs that say *Geschlossen bis ende November* ("closed 'til the end of November") and hardly an open shop to be seen.

If you do plan to restock at Zürs, note that it seems to take a longer lunch hour than other Austrian towns. Typically, shops close at 11 A.M. for two hours. Otherwise, they are generally open from 8 to 6.

The crucial navigational point about today's walk is that for the second half of it you leave the 601 and take, first, the 643 to the Stuttgarter Hütte and then the 645 southwards from there to the Ulmer Hütte. All this is because the 601 breaks mysteriously between Zürs and the village of Rauzalpe below the Ulmer Hütte. You rejoin it at the hut. The detour is not merely an expedient; it offers some very fine walking.

From the Ravensburger Hütte, follow the river valley up the mountain, keeping to the west side of the river itself. Watch for the red trail markers as they point the way up to the Stierloch Joch, taking care not to walk too far east along the line of the river valley. It is a steep but fairly short climb to this small pass, from which you can look back down to the Spüllersee and forward to the cable car station above the Zürser See. The station lies at the other end of a small, very steep valley and is reached by picking your way across the scree (and perhaps snow) along the south side.

A steep, muddy path follows the line of the cable car down to the Zürser See, an uninviting body of water that looks more like a stagnant pond than the sparkling mountain lakes you have been used to seeing. Make your way round the southern side of this small lake and find a path going southeast over a grassy hillside towards Zürs. The main road leading there is visible, as are the cable car runs on the mountains opposite.

Turn left when you reach the main road and walk a short distance into the town. Pass the post office on the left; a short way later turn right over a stream to find a car-size track that leads up towards Trittalpe. Once you find this track, there are no further navigational problems this side of the Stuttgarter Hütte. Leave a hotel to your left and follow the signs across a wide meadow from which the hut should be visible, some 350 meters above.

Cross the Pazüel Bach, going roughly northeast across the meadow, and begin the climb around the side of the valley, following a fairly obvious line of ascent. About halfway up the track turns towards the north in order to cross a stream tumbling down into the valley. The path climbs steadily upwards to reach the hut, which is on a ridge that offers fine views both east and west. Here you get your first taste of the kind of territory waiting for you in the days to come: the mountains suddenly lose much of their green mantle and become mostly barren and eroded masses where jagged rock gives way only to scree or snow.

Follow the Ulmer Hütte sign south from the Stuttgarter, and begin a walk somewhat reminiscent of the climb from the Göppinger Hütte. The path clings to the side of a valley that appears to be a huge, natural cul de sac: there is more greenery and less rock than the Göppinger climb, but there is a similar feeling of penetrating to the heart of the mountains. A snowfield at the end apparently blocks the way out.

The path is a little treacherous at times, making its way, more or less without gradient, across scree and perhaps some snow patches. The sheltered position of the snowfield at the end of the valley suggests that it is permanent and not a climatic exception. As you approach it you will find a sign pointing left to Valluga. Do not follow it; instead step onto the snow and start the long climb up to the Tritt Scharte.

The chances are the snow will be well trodden, so the way is likely to be obvious. If it is not, you should aim for a point halfway across the field's width at its narrowest point. From there you should be able to see the top and you should aim for the left-hand corner of it. This will bring you to the bottom of a steep gully, which will be your last climb for the day. The steepness of this gully and the looseness of its surface have resulted in a cable, by which you can haul yourself up, being suspended from the top. Your party should go up only one at a time because of the danger of rock falling on those below. Using your arms for a change provides a surprising advantage and you get to the top of this daunting-looking gully in no time.

From the top — little more than a tiny gap in the rock wall and a good example of the meaning of the word *Scharte* (a gap or pass) — you can see the Ulmer Hütte among a collection of buildings directly below. The way down is slow, steep, and treacherous underfoot, but it finally levels out to bring you to the hut in about half an hour.

While the Freiburger lacks real "mountain hut" flavor because of its size, the Ulmer does because of its location. Far from being a cozy timbered cabin nestling in a rocky nook somewhere, it stands in an isolated position near the bottom of a cable car run. A sign on the side of the hut warns you to watch out for explosions from local rock blasting, heralded by the activation of a flashing red light attached to the sign. However, the hut makes up for its shortcomings by providing showers — a rarity — and superb food: wonderful *Knödeln* with mushroom sauce and absolutely the best *Apfelstrudel mit schlagzahne* (apple cake with whipped cream).

DAY 7

Ulmer Hütte (2279 m) to Ansbacher Hütte (2376 m) via Leutkircher Hütte (2252 m)

> *Time:* 8 hours
> *Distance:* 20 kilometers (12.4 miles)
> *Viewpoints:* Above the Hintersee; east from the Alperschonjoch
> *Access:* Rauzalpe; St. Anton

The eastward trek from the Ulmer Hütte marks your entry into the Lechtaler Alpen proper and is the beginning of the section that runs parallel to the Inn Valley. Views of the valley and its habitations are seen quite often, but this does not mean the route is becoming more populated. This second half is more consistently spectacular and probably more physically demanding than the first. Day 7 is a fairly long walk, mostly over rocky terrain and with one or two scrambling sections.

A sign on the western side of the Ulmer Hütte points in the direction of the Leutkircher Hütte, one of today's intermediate points. The day starts with a climb of about 300 meters to a saddle where the path from Valluga comes in on your left. A few red marks on the rocks should guide you across this high section in a south-easterly direction before you descend a little to find a path across a scree slope straight along the side of the Weissschrofen Spitze.

Perhaps the best feature of today's walk is that you neither lose nor gain very much height — the range is roughly from 2200 meters to 2500 meters. The first section, to the Leutkircher, follows this pattern, going with the contours for some way after the initial climb. There are a few sharp, rocky, but short climbs. The Leutkircher Hütte is small, white, and a good place for midmorning refreshments. Sit on the bench outside and admire the view of St. Anton to the southwest.

The route to the Kaiserjoch Haus is well-marked and, in contrast to the earlier section of the walk, over grassy mountainside. Parts of it are quite steep. When you get there, you will find it's even smaller than the Leutkircher, but with a new extension on the side. The walk eastwards continues with a climb over grassland and later into some very rocky country which sets the tone for the next couple of days.

Steel cables help when the path requires a scramble up a gully. (Ian Anderson photo)

A walk along the steep and treacherous side of the Kridlon Spitze with the Hintersee below and to the left is followed by a very steep zigzag climb over loose gravel to the Hinterseejoch, nothing but a ridge of rock a few feet wide. The climb to get there looks absolutely awful from below, but as a veteran of the Hoher Freschen and the Hochschere you will probably be able to eat this one for afternoon tea.

If you are beginning to think that mountain walking has more in common with mountain climbing, the next section of the walk will confirm your suspicions. The path clings to the mountainside, marked at times only by stretches of blue nylon rope that allow you to shuffle and shin your way around some sections of rock where you cannot walk. The ropes are especially welcome anchors above some precipitous sections.

After about two hours you will find yourself at the Alperschonjoch, a pass overlooking a huge sweep of mostly barren mountains; the scene has more in common with the rocky wildernesses of the Middle East than with traditional Alpine images of green meadows, rushing streams, and tinkling cowbells.

The old roof of a hut lies in the middle of the pass, presumably to shelter walkers and climbers. It seems the efforts of whoever put it there have not been wasted, for it is full of empty bottles and cans. Next to it is a board inscribed with "601" and you should follow this southeast, passing the path signposted to the Simms Hütte on your left. Red paint on the rocks guides you up the short rocky ascent to yet another small pass, from where you can see the path leading round the mountainside and down towards the Ansbacher. Pass the path to the Memminger Hütte coming in from the left (you will have to retrace your steps to this tomorrow) and continue another five minutes around a steep, grassy mountainside until suddenly, around a corner and in the best tradition of surprise endings to the day, the Ansbacher Hütte appears.

This hut is the antithesis of the Austrian mountain-hut-as-hotel. It is old, primitive, and tiny; on a fine summer's weekend it probably contravenes every health and fire regulation in Austria. On such occasions it is packed to the gunwales with *Bergsteigers* who fled their offices and escaped into the mountains. A quiet chat with your walking companions in the corner of the *Gaststube* is out of the question. You will probably be squeezed into a seat where you will have to wait for your food order to be taken by the "hands-up" *Furglsteigergulaschbrot* system. The narrow wooden staircase creaks on your way upstairs to a room where people cram into every available space for the night. The only washing facilities appear to be a basin alongside the nonflush toilet. A German guide I met there told me it was the worst hut he knew. Alternatively, you may find it unspoiled and full of Old World charm.

DAY 8

Ansbacher Hütte (2376 m) to Memminger Hütte (2242 m) via Parseiertal (1723 m)

Time: 5 to 6 hours
Distance: 10 kilometers (6.2 miles)
Viewpoints: East from the Griesslscharte towards
the Parseiertal and the Memminger Hütte;
the climb to the Memminger
Access: The road from Bach leading to the Parseiertal

Superlatives could not do justice to today's walk, probably the most spectacular of the trip. The distance is short but the going is slow due to the difficulty of the descent.

Retrace last night's steps uphill towards the path to the Memminger. After the path branches off to the right, you will have a rocky ascent to the Winterjoch and then to the Griesslscharte. There may be snow on the way up, but the track will be obvious. From the Griesslscharte you start a perilous but spectacular descent. You can see the Memminger Hütte perched on the side of the mountain ahead of you. Below is the Parseiertal, and you may not believe that it is possible to get all the way down there, let alone climb up the other side. But it is — and it's worth it.

The descent from the pass is slow and laborious; it is made easier by cables in the rock, but requires great care both for your own safety and for those below who may be hit by loose rock. You may have some snow patches to negotiate. After you have finished creeping, sliding, and tottering down the steepest of the descent, the mountainside becomes a little more gradual and the path leads over a stream and winds, boulder-strewn, through a pine wood a short way above the river at the bottom of the Parseiertal.

The river is a delightful place for a well-earned rest after the relentless downhill your legs have just suffered. From here you have a partial view of the Zammer Parseier to the south. A 601 sign is painted in red on one of the large rocks by the river.

If you are trying not to think about the way up to the hut on the grounds that it will be the equivalent of what you have just come down, do not despair. It is a tough climb, but not as brutally long or

The route to Memminger Hütte passes through a spectacular valley. (Ian Anderson photo)

steep as the one you have just done in reverse, and it should not take you more than two hours. Find the path below some rocks on the east side of the stream and make your way along it to cross a small wooden bridge across a narrow but deep fissure in the rock. The track leads through small patches of woodland and then across grassy slopes. From here you will be able to see behind you perhaps the most memorable view of the trip: that precipitous valley between the Freispitze and the Griessl Spitze you have just scrambled down. It is magnificent.

N

0   3   6km

Nassereith

601

Innsbruck

Hinterbergjoch 2210

11
Anhalter Hütte 2042

Boden

601

Hanauer Hütte 1918

10
Steinseehütte 2030

Gufelgras-Joch

9
Memminger
Hütte 2242

Württumberger
Hütte 2220

Landeck

Parseiertal

Frei-Spitze
2887

601

8
Ansbacher
Hütte 2376

The Memminger Hütte is in a pleasant upper valley terminated abruptly to the east and south by steep mountain faces. It is
served by a cable car at the end of a road from Bach and Grunau,
making it quite accessible; at weekends it is likely to be packed.
Take advantage of the relatively short length of today's walk and get
to the hut early to grab a mattress before you get relegated to the
ranks of the *Notlager,* who must sleep on mattresses on the floor.
However, the Memminger is much better able to cope with crowds
than the Ansbacher and there is a sizeable *Gaststube.*

DAY 9

Memminger Hütte (2242 m) to Steinsee Hütte (2030 m) via
Grossberg Kopf (2657 m), Würtemberger Hütte (2220 m) and
Gufelgrasjoch (2389 m)

> *Time:* 6 to 7 hours
> *Distance:* 13 kilometers (8 miles)
> *Viewpoints:* Eastwards from the Seescharte;
> panorama from the Grossberg Kopf
> *Access:* The road from Bach leading to the Parseiertal

Today you will have a fairly strenuous walk through rocky terrain,
with some very steep climbs.

There's no point in trying to sleep through the early morning
confusion in the Memminger. As in most huts, it mysteriously
begins at about 5 A.M. and quickly rises to a crescendo of shuffling,
coughing, banging, and gurgling as everyone attempts to get his or
her act together for the day's walk. If the bathroom is unbearable or
the wait for breakfast is too long, take a break and sit outside for a
few minutes to let the crowds subside and watch the sun come up.
You cannot fail to feel serene as you watch the Griessl Spitze,
Freispitze, and Saxerspitze shade from the slightest pink-brown
tint on their nighttime silhouettes to light orange and finally to the
illumination of bright sunlight as it emerges from behind the
Kleinberg Spitze to the east. By now you should be able to face the
throng again.

The Memminger marks the convergence of the E4 route with
another trans-European footpath, the E5, and the two run together
for a couple of kilometers. A sign on the side of the hut tells you this

and points you east along this megatrail and across the valley to the Seescharte.

Apart from the brief stroll across the valley floor, this is not a gentle start to the day. The climb to the Seescharte is steep and loose and a daunting prospect from below. It may also be a little cold because you will be in the shadow of the mountain. From the pass, which is rather like the gap caused by a missing tooth, the path goes over bare, loose mountainside and leads southeast for a short way, towards a wide green valley in the direction of Landeck.

Take care not to be seduced by the beautiful view of this valley, for you must turn left after a few hundred meters at a path marked 601 and WH (Würtemberger Hütte). Both these signs are painted on rocks shortly after you have turned left. (The path straight ahead — which you should not take — is marked to Zams.) This left turn marks the reemergence of the E4. Follow a very narrow, almost level path along the steep side of the Kleinberg Spitze through a huge scree field. It is loose and only wide enough for one person, so care is needed. After this, scramble along a series of rocky ridges towards the Grossberg Spitze, the highest point on the route. On this final approach to the peak, you get a real "roof-of-the-world" feeling with a 360-degree view over the tops of endless mountains. If the weather is fine, you may see lines of other walkers silhouetted against the sky as they make their way along the ridge.

From the Grossberg Spitze, you can see the Würtemberger Hütte, a tiny building amid a rocky wilderness. It looks very close, but it's at least an hour away. The initial descent is quite dangerous, with a very steep, loose surface and an ill-defined path, parts of which have to be scrambled rather than walked down, with the aid of cables. A small shortcut at the beginning of the descent, immediately below the summit, should be avoided due to the danger of dislodging rock. After the trauma of all this there is a pleasant, mostly grassy run-in to the Würtemberger, where you can lunch outside as a stream gurgles past after having done its work in the mini hydroelectric plant above the hut.

Leaving the Würtemberger, you must climb steeply for about fifteen minutes onto a small saddle from which a small lake is visible. Continue up to the Gebäudjochl, from where you can see the Steinsee Hütte, your destination.

The second of the afternoon's three passes, the Gufelgrasjoch, is very tough indeed. It looks a sheer wall from below and is —

almost. The way up, only just discernible on the loose scree, zigzags over the lower part of the climb and then disappears for the last 100 meters or so, which is essentially a rock face. Cables hanging down the rock make the going easier, but the metal handholds on them are too far apart, leading to a few desperate lunges as you battle to haul yourself up. The reward at the top is a thin ridge of rock from which you can see the path ahead leading along the side of a very rocky and barren valley with a small lake at the bottom of it. The path gets narrow and rather precipitous, taking you to a small *Scharte* that is the last obstacle before the final descent to the hut. These last couple of kilometers are pleasant, the mountainside acquiring a green covering with a gorgeous pink spattering of azaleas.

The Steinsee Hütte feels more isolated than many of the other huts. It is small and pleasant and has recently been redecorated. Its only problem is the lack of light in the dorms, which can make going to bed very difficult if you don't have a flashlight. Above the hut is the Steinsee itself, which I am told provides "invigorating" bathing. However icy the waters of this and similar wayside lakes are, you may find this is not enough to deter you from immersion when the opportunity arises.

Steep descent from the Grossberg Kopf, toward Steinsee Hütte (Ian Anderson photo)

DAY 10

Steinsee Hütte (2030 m) to Anhalter Hütte (2042 m) via Hanauer Hütte (1918 m) and Boden (1357 m)

Time: 6 hours
Distance: 15 kilometers (9.3 miles)
Viewpoints: South from west Dremel Scharte
Access: Boden

This is a pleasant and moderate day's walk, with the exception of the first half hour, which is a decidedly rude awakening.

From the Steinsee Hütte, follow the signs to the Hanauer Hütte. The ground rises fairly steeply as you wind up the grassy mountainside towards the Steinsee itself. Shortly below it, the path forks and you must take the left path, marked 601, to the west Dremel Scharte. The way up is comparable in severity to yesterday's Gufelgrasjoch, although perhaps not quite as steep. It has loose scree at the bottom and solid rock at the top; the final 200 meters is assisted by cables. The ascent needs some care to avoid dislodging rocks and some thought to find the most efficient way up.

You can see the Hanauer Hütte from the *Scharte,* which belies the usual definition of the word by actually being big enough to sit down on for a rest. The descent to the hut is not very easy to begin with, passing over loose scree before getting onto grass as you approach the hut. Even if you are tired of descending scree slopes, you should relish this one because it marks the real descent from the mountains into gentler and more inhabited country. The large number of signs at the hut indicates that the area is much frequented by walkers and the path down from the hut, being exceptionally well maintained, confirms this.

The track leads into the valley, past the lower cable car station serving the hut, and onto a car-size track over meadows and through pine woods to Boden. This is a pleasant village evidently much used as a departure point for the mountains. You will be seeing cars, shops, and houses for the first time since Zürs, four days ago.

Make your way to the upper end of the village, pass a shop, and then leave the road at a point near a bridge on your right, following the 601 signs. A sign on a barn by the bridge says it's three and a half hours to the Anhalter Hütte. The track winds up through fields and woods and latterly by a stream to join a main road where you turn right. You must endure perhaps a kilometer of road walking here, guided by two red-painted 601 signs: one on a rock opposite the point where you join the road and the other on the roadside wall a little further along. Go past a *Gasthaus* and a roadside cafe and leave the road at the first hairpin bend you come to, once again following red signs on the rocks.

A muddy, rocky path leads up by the side of a stream and on to a meadow by the side of the road you have just left. Hit the road again for about 200 meters and then follow a flashy roadside sign up the mountain to the Anhalter. Climb up the side of the Heiterwand along a wide and very well-worn path. From the top, marked by a large crucifix, it is only fifteen minutes down an easy track to the hut. This is a bona fide mountain hut, but it advertises itself like a hotel and that fact is, I'm afraid, one indication that the end of your walk is nigh.

DAY 11

Anhalter Hütte (2042 m) to Nassereith (850 m) via Kromsattel (2201 m), Hinter Tarrenton Alpe (1541 m) and the Tegestal

> *Time:* 6 hours
> *Distance:* 16 kilometers (9.92 miles)
> *Viewpoints:* Eastward from the Kromsattel; the Tegestal
> *Access:* The road below the Anhalter; Nassereith

This is an easy walk, heading downhill along good tracks, with the exception of the Kromsattel. It begins with a steady climb up a small spur of the Heiterwand from the hut. Follow the 601 signs outside the hut along a track that runs parallel to a stream and then climbs steeply to a saddle. From here you look over a scree-covered valley. Do not head straight down the valley, but go across the scree, descending somewhat across the western end of the valley, but not losing too much height. Red marks on the rocks point to the eastern edge of the scree slope where the mountainside becomes grassy again. Look carefully for a bent red arrow painted on a small rock face. It indicates the beginning of a short but steep zigzag

"Supply line" brings food and beer to the huts. (Ian Anderson photo)

climb to the Kromsattel. From this pleasant grassy ridge below the Heiterwand you can see the valley that begins the final descent to Nassereith.

The next hour or so is the last real mountain walking you will do and is slow and difficult. The path is not steep for the most part, but is littered with large rocks, which need care, especially if the day is wet. Halfway down the valley a sign on your right indicates the high route to the Heiterwand Hütte. Stay on the 601 and continue down the valley, less steeply now, past a small farm and then to a larger farm at Hinter Tarrenton Alpe.

With this final approach to the valley at Nassereith you are well and truly out of the mountains, but the landscape provides some fine woodland on gentle gradients. From Hinter Tarrenton Alpe, follow 601 signs east and after a time pass on the right the route to the Heiterwand Hütte. The track is a logging road and winds easily downhill next to and sometimes considerably above a rushing stream. About 1 kilometer before Nassereith you pass a barrier across the track. There is a cabin near here and a path to the left to Fernstein.

Stay on the track leading downhill toward the main road between Nassereith and Imst. Turn right within sight of the main road and follow a woodland track roughly parallel to the road for about twenty minutes. About halfway there a yellow sign points the way to Nassereith. Pass some houses and before long you are on the main road. A few hundred meters down the road to your right are a group of shops and a bus terminal where you can get buses to Innsbruck or the Inn Valley, where you can pick up trains going west.

⌒~ *TOUR 2* ~⌒

Rätikon/Silvretta

Route: *(Bludenz) – Douglass Hütte –*
Lindauer Hütte – Tilisuna Hütte –
Gargellen/Madrisa Hütte – Tübinger Hütte –
Wiesbadener Hütte – Jamtal Hütte – Ischgl

The Rätikon and Silvretta mountain groups are neighbors in the far
southwest of Austria. The Rätikon runs east to west, ending at the
Rhine Valley near Liechtenstein and Sargans, while the Silvretta
stretches east and south, straddling the Austro-Swiss border and
running into the Samnaungruppe southwest of Landeck.

The major peaks of the Rätikon include the Sulzfluh (2818
meters), Schesaplana (2985 meters), and the Madrisa Horn (2826
meters). All are part of the ridge that forms Austria's border with
Switzerland in this region. The Silvretta's tops are somewhat higher
than the Rätikon; they include the Grosser Litzner (3109 meters), the
Silvretta Horn (3244 meters), Piz Buin (3312 meters), Fluchthorn
(3399 meters), Augsten Spitz (3228 meters), and Dreiländer Spitz
(3197 meters).

The route described here starts in the Rätikon and roughly
follows the border ridge, going southeast to the Silvretta region, then
turning northeast to end at Ischgl, north of the Samnaungruppe. It is

For walkers of the Rätikon/Silvretta route, Ischgl is journey's end. (Tyrolean   55
National Tourist Office, Innsbruck, photo)

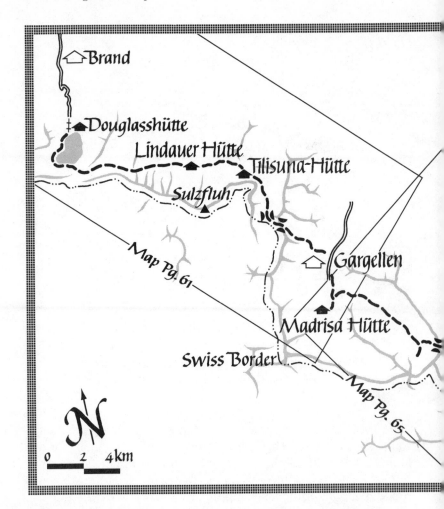

an eight-day tour, mostly consisting of short hops between huts; you will have time for detouring, climbing peaks, or simply sunning yourself. Trails are well marked and well trodden, this being a very popular walkers' region. Gradients are very steep at times, but nothing in this route should bother reasonably fit walkers with ordinary equipment. There is no technical climbing.

The territory through which you will walk will be mostly fertile mountainside, supporting grasses and wild flowers, plus a few trees and shrubs. The higher stretches will be rocky and largely barren, with the possibility of snow in a few places. Whatever the conditions

underfoot, you will be treated to a constant array of stunningly beautiful mountain scenery. On many a hard climb you will pause for breath to look up at a vast rocky peak, down on a green land of matchbox-size farms and fields, or out over a seemingly endless panorama of Alpine peaks, many of them snow-covered. Yes, a hutting trip in the Alps requires stamina, but its rewards are immense.

Maps: Freytag and Berndt 1:100,000 No. 37 Rätikon, Silvretta und Verwallgruppe.

DAY 1

Douglass Hütte (1979 m) to Lindauer Hütte (1744 m) via Schweizertor (2137 m)

Time: 4.5 hours
Distance: 12 kilometers (7.44 miles)
Viewpoints: Schweizertor
Access: Bludenz

This half-day walk has no serious climbs but you'll cross two passes and have some good views, particularly of the Lüner See. You will spend the first couple of hours on public transport, getting to the Douglass Hütte.

The starting point is Bludenz, from whose railway station you can get a bus past Brand to the cable car station below the Douglass Hütte. A route from Brand to the cable car is walkable, but it runs very close to the road for some of the way and actually on the road at the end, so it is best to stay on the bus until the end of its run. It is also possible to walk up from the bottom of the cable car to the hut, but this seems an unfairly strenuous start to your holiday, so I recommend taking the cable car.

At the Douglass Hütte, go around the western side of the Lüner See, following signs to the Lindauer Hütte. This is a pleasant, level walk and will be very crowded on weekends. Stay fairly close to the lakeside until you are opposite the Douglass Hütte on the other side of the lake. Here, at a farm, turn right, up towards the Kirchlispitzen. This path is the Rätikon-Höhenweg Nord and is marked 102. It takes you over some grassy mountainside and up beside the Kirchlispitzen to the Verajöchli, the first of the day's passes. Looking back, you have an impressive view of the Schesaplana, one of the highest points of the Rätikon.

The track towards the Lindauer should be clear from this pass, running down over grassland to the Schweizertor and up again the other side of the valley to the Öfapass. The Schweizertor was evidently once a Swiss border post; all that remains is a deserted customs house. A short way south of the path, a tall yellow sign and a small stone obelisk mark the Swiss-Austrian border.

There is a long descent to the Lindauer Hütte after the next pass and you walk below the Drusenfluh and the Drei Türme. Part way down you will see a black metal plaque set into a rock below

Luner See, near Douglass Hütte (Richard Cox photo)

the forbidding-looking Drusenfluh, commemorating a climber who was killed on that mountain in 1946. Victims of the mountains are often honored in this way, a somber reminder of the danger and indifference of the mountains.

The Lindauer, which you can see from above, is an excellent first-night hut. The night I was there it was in full cry — literally. A trio of singers had arrived for the evening and was leading the entire population of the *Gaststube* in a seemingly endless repertoire of traditional Tyrolean tunes.

DAY 2

Lindauer Hütte (1744 m) to Tilisuna Hütte (2208 m), with a round trip to the Sulzfluh (2818 m)

> *Time:* 3 hours to hut; allow 4.5 hours
> for round trip from hut to Sulzfluh
> *Distance:* 5 kilometers (3 miles)
> *Viewpoints:* Sulzfluh; the climb away from the Lindauer
> *Access:* Road from Schruns

This is a half-day walk to the next hut and then a full afternoon's trek to the summit of one of the highest peaks in the Rätikon. Much of the route to the hut is steep and twisting but the climb to the Sulzfluh is more gradual and scenically more rewarding.

Follow the signs outside the Lindauer to the Tilisuna. The path heads downhill and through a pine wood for about half a kilometer. You emerge from the trees to cross an open valley, then climb steeply up its left side. This is the beginning of a twisting path that is unrelentingly steep and will take you about one and a half hours to climb. There are good views overlooking the valley containing the Lindauer, and views of the path you took to get to the Lindauer yesterday. If you are surrounded by clouds, as I was on making this ascent, they may blow away occasionally to reveal tantalizing glimpses of the mountains. The clouds swirl capriciously up and down the valley, uncovering for a moment a peak, some scree, or a grassy slope and then swallowing it up again. These fleeting glimpses added to the magic of the mountains.

The Tilisuna Hütte is not visible from the pass at the top of the climb but it is only twenty minutes away down a narrow track over the grassy mountainside. The hut is a good base for the trip to the Sulzfluh, which has the reputation of being one of the best viewpoints in the Rätikon. It is well worth doing, but it is a full afternoon's walk and although you will probably want to leave your rucksacks at the hut, you should take sufficient sustenance for a strenuous trek.

The signs to the Sulzfluh direct you steeply up in a southwesterly direction. The climb up over grassy mountainside leads abruptly onto a rocky limestone plateau. You can see the Sulzfluh, with a crucifix on its summit, directly in front of you and with a large snowfield below it and to the right. This is a well-trodden route and is marked with cairns the whole way to the snowfield. The cairns head southwest and follow a line that dips slightly before climbing the main massif of the mountain. As the path begins to climb again, notice the cairns along the ridge above and briefly turn south to join the ridge before continuing southwest towards the summit.

The sheer walls of the summit prevent you from approaching it from the east, so you have to head for the snowfield and work your way around to attack the peak from the other side. The snow should be well trodden and perfectly navigable for walkers wearing ordinary boots. From the top of the snowfield, it is just a short climb to the summit. At the base the cross is a small metal box containing an ink pad and a rubber stamp, a simple but smart way for climbers to embellish their maps to prove they have been to the summit.

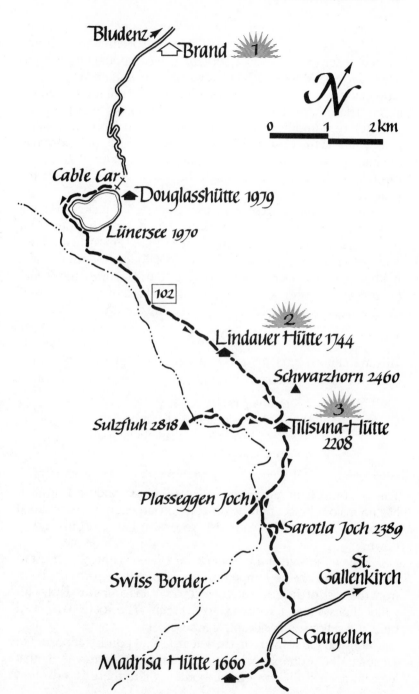

Bludenz

Brand 1

N

0   1   2km

Cable Car

Douglasshütte 1979

Lünersee 1970

102

2

Lindauer Hütte 1744

Schwarzhorn 2460

Sulzfluh 2818

3

Tilisuna-Hütte 2208

Plasseggen Joch

Sarotla Joch 2389

St. Gallenkirch

Swiss Border

Gargellen

Madrisa Hütte 1660

Also on the summit is a notice asking you not to write on the cross. To cater to the possibly justifiable urge of climbers to leave a written record of their achievement, a local mountain club has erected a large wooden lattice on which a great many *Bergsteigers* have made their mark. This is not a pretty sight, but it is preferable to the defaced crucifix that would be the probable alternative.

Before tramping back to the hut, visit the mountain's other peak, a little to the west, which shows much more dramatically than the main peak the enormous sheer drop to the south. *Vorsicht* (be careful)! Trek back down through the soft snow before retracing your steps along the rocky road back to the hut.

The Tilisuna Hütte seemed to me somewhat characterless: it was apparently recently modernized, with not much thought for preserving the old woody atmosphere found in so many huts. Authoritarian signs around the hut do not endear themselves and neither does the lack of a pudding at dinner, surely the weary *Bergsteiger*'s "just desserts" at the end of a hard day.

DAY 3

Tilisuna Hütte (2208 m) to Gargellen (1423 m)/Madrisa Hütte (1660 m) via the Sarotla Joch (2389 m)

*Time:*4.5 hours
*Distance:*10 kilometers (6.2 miles)
*Viewpoints:*Sarotla Joch; Plasseggen Joch
*Access:*Gargellen

This is an excellent morning's walk with some wonderful views. It has no major climbs, but the descent to Gargellen — nearly 1,000 meters — might make you wish you were going up instead of down.

Follow the sign at the front of the Tilisuna Hütte southeast to Gargellen. Do not be tempted to go south on the path that leads from the back of the hut. The correct path leads over grassland with white limestone outcroppings to the right. The route is marked blue and yellow on rocks and signposts.

You will pass a path on the left at a small pond, signposted to Tilisuna Alpe. Continue straight on, climbing a narrow gully that leads to a small *Scharte* on the border where there is a disused customs hut and several metal signs fixed to the rock. Through the gap you can see, to the west, the Sulzfluh with its cross. Make a sharp left turn and walk down along the steep side of the valley below the Weissplatte. Make your way into a glorious broad valley where the path rises gently over grassland to the Plasseggen Joch. Here you will be rewarded by great views to both east and west.

Take the track signposted to Gargellen that goes along the side of the Sarotla Spitze. Around a bend, you will suddenly behold the Sarotla Joch, an attractive pass made spectacular by the view of the jagged snowy peaks of the Silvretta to the southeast. The ground slopes steeply to the east and a peak towers overhead on either side of you. This is one of the places that will endure in your memory of the Alps.

At the pass, the track marks turn to red and white. The track is well marked, and zigzags steeply down for much of the way. Gargellen, with its brilliant blue swimming pool, is visible below about an hour before you get there. When you reach the treeline, turn right, following a sign to Gargellen. Go through the woods and finally onto the road, a welcome respite for your legs after the jarring descent.

Gargellen is a typical valley village and survives mostly on tourism, both summer and winter. It's very neat and you may wish to take advantage of the swimming pool after a couple of days in huts with no showers. If you decide to stay at the Madrisa Hütte, you must get the key from Haus Wulfenia, a large guest house just a couple of minutes' walk from the post office/supermarket in the center of the village. To get there, head down the hill from the post office and take the first right turn, over the river. Turn left on the other side, and the house, with its name painted in large letters, is straight in front of you. You will be asked to surrender your Alpine Club card, which will be returned the next morning when you bring the key back — and pay. (Bringing the key back involves retracing steps before starting the journey to the Tübinger tomorrow; you may wish to save time by staying in Gargellen.)

To get to Madrisa Hütte, go south out of Gargellen. The road climbs gradually, and at a point about 400 meters beyond the chairlift that crosses the road, there is a track on the right with signs pointing to the Madrisa and other places. Follow this winding timber road for about forty minutes, until you get well away from the village. A low farmhouse becomes visible on the other side of the valley and shortly after this you should see a sign on the right pointing to other huts. Take the track opposite this sign on the left side of the road and you will see the Madrisa immediately below among the trees.

The hut is very pleasant and woody. A small stream bubbles past just to one side of the hut (it supplies the water) and a much larger stream tumbles down the valley in front. The hut has no warden but is well equipped in kitchen and dormitories. Despite the lack of a warden it was one of the most expensive I visited in the summer of 1985; this could prove another reason to seek a bed in one of Gargellen's guest houses instead.

Alternate route: Gargellen is the only town you visit between the Douglass Hütte and Ischgl, a fact worth bearing in mind since it is a viable escape route if the weather turns nasty. You can take a bus from here down the valley to St. Gallenkirch and from there to Bielerhöhe and the Silvretta Stausee. You can start here again later if the weather improves; meanwhile the valley towns give you the opportunity to stock up on food, film, adhesive dressings, and other necessities.

DAY 4

Gargellen (1423 m)/Madrisa Hütte (1660 m) to Tübinger Hütte (2191 m) via Vergalda Tal and the Vergaldner Joch (2515 m) plus a round-trip climb of the Hochmaderer (2823 m)

Time: 4.5 hours, plus 2.5 hours for the summit
climb round trip
Distance: 10.5 kilometers (6.5 miles)
Viewpoints: Hochmaderer
Access: Gargellen or Gaschurn

This is a full morning's walk to the hut, with the option of climbing the Hochmaderer in the afternoon. The overall climb to the Vergaldner Joch is about 1,000 meters and most of the distance is steadily up the Vergalda Tal, followed by a sharp climb to the pass and then down the other side some 400 meters to the hut.

The day starts with an easy walk up the Vergalda Tal. The path starts from the gravel road above Gargellen and is on the right if you are returning down the valley after spending the night at the

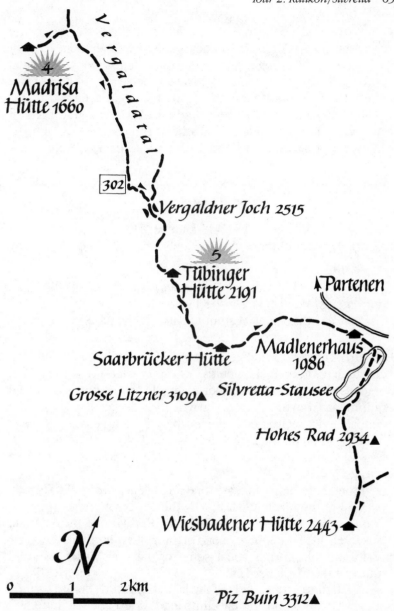

Madrisa Hütte. It is a well-made, car-size track, number 302, that will take you to Vergalda Alpe about half way up the valley. From here, keep going straight up the valley, but on a smaller track.

At the end of the valley turn left and climb steeply to the Vergaldner Joch. Continue southeast and to another ridge; from it you can see the Tübinger Hütte some 300 meters below. The final approach to the hut contours around the lower slopes of the Kessihorn to the hut itself at the head of the Garnertal.

The afternoon can be spent climbing the Hochmaderer. A path leaves the Tübinger Hütte in a northerly direction and then turns east to climb the Hochmaderer Joch with a final scramble to the peak.

DAY 5

Tübinger Hütte (2191 m) to Wiesbadener Hütte (2443 m) via the Saarbrücker Hütte (2538 m) and the Silvretta Stausee (2034 m)

Time: 7 hours
Distance: 18 kilometers (11.16 miles)
Viewpoints: Many; this is a spectacular walk
Access: Garnertal/Vermunt Stausee/Silvretta Stausee

Leave the Tübinger Hütte going southeast, and climb to the Platten Scharte across some snowfields. You must then cross two small stretches of glacier; they are perfectly safe and require no special equipment. From the glaciers you will have spectacular views of the Seehorn and the Grosse Litzner, both to the southeast.

Turn south off the ridge that has afforded you these views and descend slightly from the glaciers to reach the Saarbrücker Hütte on route 302.

From here it is an easy one-and-a-half-hour walk steadily downhill to the Madlener Haus, by the road that comes up from Partenen. This hut is directly beneath the dam of the Silvretta Stausee. Head to the southern end of this reservoir, where it may be possible to take a motorboat some of the way. Walkers should inquire at the Madlener Haus.

Continue along the side of the lake southwards before turning southeast to make the gradual climb to the Wiesbadener Hütte. You will climb about 400 meters in the generous space of about 5.6 kilometers.

There are very good views of the glaciers and the frontier ridge to the south from the Wiesbadener Hütte. It is very popular for day trips, but will be quieter in the evening.

Silvretta Hütte (Cecil Davies photo)

Alternate Route: From the Saarbrücker Hütte, a challenging three-
to four-day loop to the south can be made by walkers who are
prepared for glacier crossings and steep gradients. It should only
be attempted in good weather. The route is: Saarbrücker Hütte –
Schweizer Lücke – Seetal Hütte – Alpe Sardasca – Silvretta Hütte –
Rota'Furka – Klosterpass – Litzner Scharte – Saarbrücker Hütte.

DAY 6

Wiesbadener Hütte (2443 m) to Jamtal Hütte (2165 m) via Radsattel
(2652 m) and Getschner Scharte (2839 m). Summit climb: Hohes
Rad (2934 m)

Time: 5 hours, including summit climb
Distance: 8 kilometers (4.96 miles)
Viewpoints: Hohes Rad; Getschner Scharte
Access: Jamtal/Bielerhöhe

This fairly strenuous walk takes a circuitous route over the ridge
west of the Jamtal. It avoids the glaciers that lie on a direct line
between the two huts. There are, however, two other routes, both
of which cross glaciers and should not be attempted without the
right experience, equipment, and guidance.

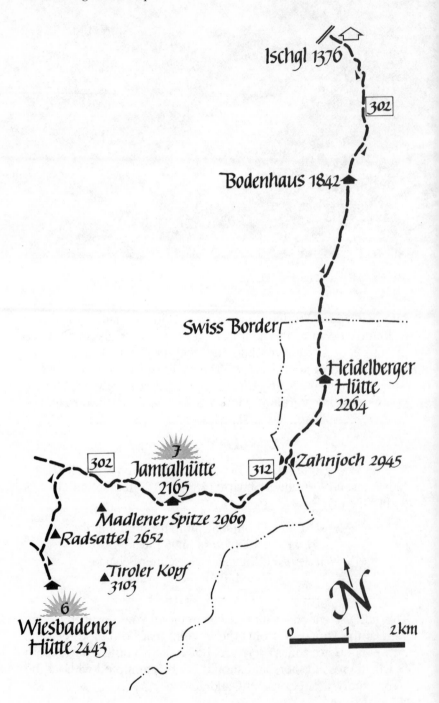

Ischgl 1376

302

Bodenhaus 1842

Swiss Border

Heidelberger
Hütte
2264

302   Jamtalhütte
7   2165

312   Zahnjoch 2945

Madlener Spitze 2969

Radsattel 2652

Tiroler Kopf
3103

6
Wiesbadener
Hütte 2443

N

0   1   2km

Take the better-trodden route north from the Wiesbadener Hütte, following an easy path for a climb of only about 200 meters to the Radsattel. The 300-meter ascent from here to the Hohes Rad will reward you with wonderful 360-degree views. The detour from the saddle takes about an hour.

Descend from the saddle and cross a small stream near the Radsee. About 0.8 kilometer after the stream crossing, branch right and begin the climb to the Getschner Scharte, one of the highest points on the route. It has good views of the major peak, the Fluchthorn, to the east and of the glaciers to the south. The 700-meter descent to the Jamtal Hütte is steep and dramatic.

DAY 7

Jamtal Hütte (2165 m) to Ischgl (1376 m) via Zahnjoch (2945 m), Heidelberger Hütte (2264 m) and the Fimbatal

> *Time:* 7 hours
> *Distance:* 20 kilometers (12.4 miles)
> *Viewpoints:* Zahnjoch
> *Access:* Jamtal/Fimbatal

This final walk is a long one, climbing the Zahnjoch, the highest point on the tour, and crossing into and out of Switzerland before heading down to the journey's end.

You face a heavy climb of some 800 meters from the Jamtal Hütte to the Zahnjoch. Take the 302 track up the Futschöl Valley east from the hut for about 3.22 kilometers and then leave the valley, turning northeast on the 312 towards the Zahnjoch, which is just south of the Fluchthorn. This pass marks the Swiss/Austrian border and the route stays in Switzerland during the easy descent to the Heidelberger Hütte. There you rejoin the 302 northwards for the long, steady descent of about 900 meters into Ischgl. Here you will be able to board a bus to Landeck, which is on the main railway line east and west.

～ TOUR 3 ～

The Ötztaler Alps
Gepatsch Haus to Sölden

Route: *Gepatsch Haus – Taschachhaus –*
Mittelberg – Braunschweiger Hütte –
(round trip to Rhein-Pfalz Biwakschachtel) – Sölden

The Ötztaler Alps, a high and extensively glaciated region touching on the Italian border southwest of Innsbruck, contain several major peaks, including the Weisskugel (3736 meters), the Glockturm (3353 meters), and Austria's second-highest mountain, the Wildspitze (3772 meters). The area is popular with climbers, skiers, and walkers, and has a good network of footpaths going past and in some cases through some spectacularly glaciated areas.

Tours 3 and 4 take full advantage of the high altitude of the region, frequently going up above 3000 meters. While the height itself should not deter most people, the amount of work needed to get there is considerable. Walkers thinking about tackling the Ötztaler Alps should be prepared for unrelentingly steep ascents of 1000 meters or more. Both routes are additionally demanding because they pass over stretches of glacier and perhaps snow.

Braunschweiger Hütte, shown here in winter, occupies a magnificent position among the glaciers of the Otztal. (Tyrolean National Tourist Office, Innsbruck, photo)

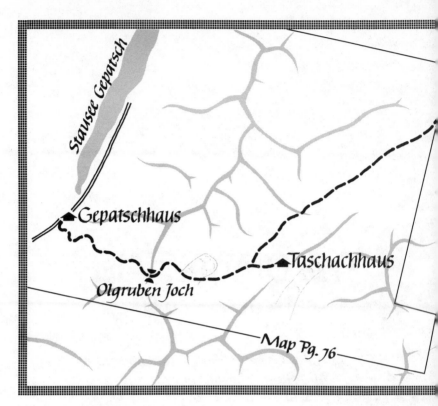

The following tour is a brief but strenuous west-east crossing of the northern part of the region. It starts from the Gepatsch Haus in the Kaunertal, south of Landeck, and visits the Taschachhaus,

Approaching the Olgruben Joch after summer snow (Richard Cox photo)

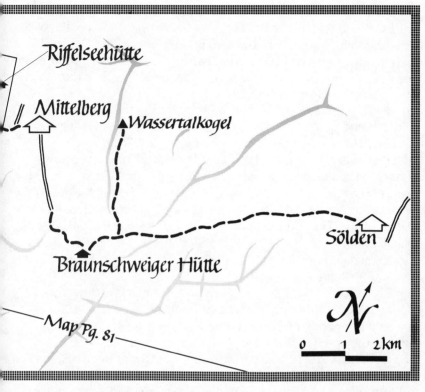

Mittelberg, the Braunschweiger Hütte, and finally Sölden, three or four days later.

Map: Wanderkarte No. 43, Ötztaler Alpen.

DAY 1

Gepatsch Haus (1928 m) to Taschachhaus (2434 m) via Ölgruben-joch (3095 m)

> *Time:* 7 hours
> *Distance:* 8 kilometers (4.96 miles)
> *Viewpoints:* Ölgrubenjoch
> *Access:* Landeck/Kaunertal

Start this trip in Landeck, on the main railway line west from Innsbruck. Buses run from here down the Oberinntal and then down the Kaunertal, the southern end of which is where the walk begins. Board the bus at the Landeck station or in the center of town, then change at Prutz and take another bus to the Gepatsch Haus at the southern end of the Stausee Gepatsch, an unlovely reservoir at the southern end of the Kaunertal. The bus journey takes about one and a half hours.

The Gepatsch Haus is clearly signposted as the bus climbs a hairpin bend going away from the southern end of the reservoir. You need not go to the Gepatsch Haus itself, but it is just a couple of minutes' walk from the road and could be useful for buying provisions or sustaining yourself before a very hard climb. When you are ready to start the climb, a sign on the left side of the road about 30 meters south of the hut drive points to the Ölgrubenjoch and the Taschachhaus. The route number on the sign (31) does not agree with the number on the Kompass Wanderkarte, but the path is clear enough and you now begin the long climb to the Ölgrubenjoch at just over 3000 meters.

The track to the pass hardly deviates from its direct ascent of the Kaunergrat, although it zigzags grudgingly from time to time. The walker spends much of the time looking down at the same view of the intestinelike road going south from the end of the Stausee Gepatsch. The track is loose, rocky, and wet in places, but well marked with red stripes on rocks. The mountainside seems well populated with marmots and you may see Alpine accentors and the less common snow bunting, which is conspicuous by its white wing markings and likely to be seen in small flocks.

There may be snow on the upper stretches of the climb but there should still be enough red marks to guide you. It will take about four hours to get to the Ölgrubenjoch, where you will find a small wooden cross just above the pass. It should be possible to see the Taschachhaus from here, as it is situated on the right-hand side of the valley far below you as it narrows into the Sexegertenbach. Actually, the hut seems to blend in with the mountains (as it should) and I was unable to see it until we came much closer.

A compass bearing of about 75 degrees will put you on course for the hut, but you should *not* attempt to walk a straight line from the pass, because of a small cliff shortly below it. This is particularly important if there is snow, which may conceal the drop. Instead, traverse to the left and make your way over a small spur and then down more steeply to the broad valley. This leads to a small lake and some presumably meteorological apparatus: a tripod marked

Looking back towards the Olgruben Joch from Taschachhaus (Richard Cox photo)

on the map as an "ombrometer." Leave the lake to your right and continue down the center of the valley, passing the end of the glacier and crossing a river to climb slightly in the final approach to the hut. Pass the path to the Riffelsee Hütte to your left shortly before reaching the Taschachhaus. This is a trying descent; the trail leads across an enormous boulder field. Do not hurry and keep a careful eye on the red markers, which point out the least awkward route through this natural junkyard and keep you away from the glacier whose icy tongue sticks down into the valley.

Your fatigue by the time you reach the Taschachhaus should not prevent you from admiring the Taschachferner, the glacier that tumbles savagely down towards the hut. The mass of huge ice boulders is divided by equally huge crevasses easily visible above the hut. It is the first real taste of glacier-scape this trip and is the more spectacular for that. What you see outside sets the scene inside the hut, which, the large number of ice axes and crampons

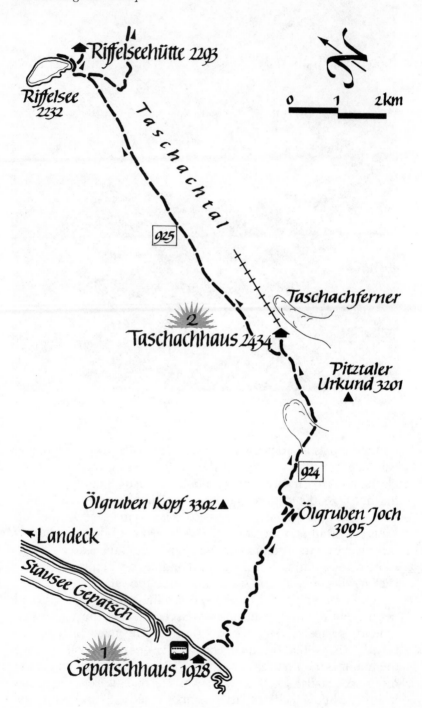

Riffelseehütte 2293

Riffelsee 2232

Taschachtal

925

Taschachferner

2 Taschachhaus 2434

Pitztaler Urkund 3201

924

Ölgruben Kopf 3392 ▲

Ölgruben Joch 3095

Landeck

Stausee Gepatsch

1 Gepatschhaus 1928

0 1 2km

inside the front door will tell you, is used by more climbers than walkers. This hut is a major center for ice climbs and multiday circuits of the local glaciers, so you are likely to be sharing your table in the *Gaststube* with mountain climbers, of the kind that get up at 4:30 A.M. and spend the day clinging to ice walls. The hut has a very hot drying room and hot showers for which there is an extra charge.

DAY 2

Taschachhaus (2434 m) to Braunschweiger Hütte (2759 m) via Mittelberg (1734 m)

> *Time:* 7 hours
> *Distance:* 14 kilometers (8.68 miles)
> *Viewpoints:* Taschachtal; Braunschweiger Hütte
> *Access:* Mittelberg

This is a variation on yesterday in that it is a long way down and then even further up again. However, much of the first half of the walk stays roughly level along the north side of the Taschachtal before descending steeply to Mittelberg. The climb to the hut is steep but spectacular, climbing by the side of a waterfall for part of the way and with a good view of a glacier further up.

From the Taschachhaus, head back toward the line of yesterday's descent but lower down and cross a plank bridge over the river next to a small pumping station. The route from here along the north side of the valley is very clear and easy walking, although one section has chains set into the rock. It is very well trodden and obviously popular with local people who drive to Mittelberg and then take day trips to one of the huts in the vicinity. The track leads to a point at the end of the Riffelsee at which the Riffelsee Hütte should be visible a short way above to the east. Unless you cannot wait for lunch, do not go to this hut, but take the track signposted to Mittelberg, about thirty minutes away down a steep twisting track. There is a cafe at the bottom of the path, at the beginning of the track down into Mittelberg. Continue down the track for a short way and then cut across a meadow behind the hotels at Mittelberg, aiming for a bridge across the river.

Walk up the paved road for a short way past the hotels and onto an unpaved but car-sized track towards the cafe at Gletscherstübele.

En route from Taschachhaus to Riffelsee Hütte (Richard Cox photo)

At the bottom go past a sign saying you are on European long distance footpath E5. This stretch of track would be rather monotonous if not for the glorious view in front of you as you walk up the valley: The Grabkogel and the Karles-Kopf tower above you on either side of the valley and a waterfall that could have been the subject of a Victorian landscape twists and thunders into the valley. At Gletscherstübele the track ends and you continue up along a rocky track towards the waterfall. It is well marked with red at this stage, but further up the painters seem to have been carried away with their task and the route is peppered with their marks. Someone has even seen fit to tell us — in huge red letters — at a point where the edge of a glacier dominates the view above, that this is a *Gletscher Blick* (glacier view). This is ironic in a country where graffiti on public buildings is almost unknown.

More of the glacier comes into view as you climb, and some stretches of the track become boulder scrambles. The hut suddenly appears above as you round the corner of the mountain. The final fifteen to twenty minutes is very steep.

The Braunschweiger Hütte is a fine resting place after a hard day. If you were exhausted by the final twist of the climb, you may collapse onto the terrace of the hut to look out onto the expanse of the Mittelbergferner with the Wildspitze in the distance and the Karlesferner stretching to the top of the Linker Ferner-Kogel directly above the hut. A track leads up to it from a point near the hut and you may see roped parties trudging slowly upwards. The proximity and extent of the glaciers give the Braunschweiger a special feel and it is ample reward for the effort you have made to get there. Like the Taschachhaus, this hut is a center for ice climbing and glacier walking and you may see parties of young people being instructed in those skills. Tempting as these glaciers might be, they should not be ventured onto without the right experience and equipment (*i.e.* crampons, ice axes, and ropes). A glacier crevasse would not be an amusing place to fall into.

The inside of the hut is the genuine article: all dark wood and rickety floorboards with a large *Gaststube* looking out on two sides to the glaciers and on another to a snow-covered mountain face.

Wildspitze and glacier from Braunschweiger Hütte (Richard Cox photo)

Alternate routes: A one- or two-day variation can be made to this tour by detouring at the Riffelsee on Day 2 and heading north to the Kaunergrat Hütte, then northeast via the Madatschjoch and the Verpeil Hütte to Feichten in the Kaunertal.

A tough but very rewarding addition to the latter part of this tour is a major extension of the trek from the Braunschweiger Hütte to the Wassertalkogel on Day 3. From the Wassertalkogel, the route runs north to the Weissmaurachjoch, passing the Chemnitzer Hütte, Sandjoch, Felderjöchl, Frischmann Hütte, Erlanger Hütte, and ending at the Hochzeiger Hütte above the village of Jerzens. The walk from the Braunschweiger Hütte should take between three and five days and should only be attempted by well-equipped, experienced, physically fit parties.

DAY 3

Braunschweiger Hütte (2759 m) to Biwakschachtel, and Wassertalkogel (3247 m) round trip via Pitztaler Jöchl, Wildes Mannle (3063 m) and Gschrappkogel (3191 m)

> *Time:* To Biwak, 4.5 hours;
>   back to Braunschweiger Hütte, 3.75 hours
> *Distance:* 9 kilometers (5.58 miles)
> *Viewpoints:* Continuous along ridge
> *Access:* Sölden

This walk takes advantage of the position of the Braunschweiger Hütte to make a challenging ridge walk visiting three peaks of over 3000 meters. Although the distance involved is small in relation to the time it takes, the going is tricky and much of the route is a scramble rather than a walk. Proper boots must be worn. The walk should not be attempted if the weather is doubtful, for it could be quite dangerous in poor visibility conditions. In good weather, you will be rewarded by 360-degree views of the glacier field and the Wildspitze to the southwest, of the mountains on the western side of the Ötztaler Alps, and of the Stubai range to the east. This walk assumes you will be staying a second night at the Braunschweiger.

Follow the signs to Sölden from the hut, climbing steadily northeast to the Pitztaler Jöchl, at very nearly 3000 meters. One of the area's many chair lifts comes up here and below you can see the parking area that accommodates the massive local ski industry

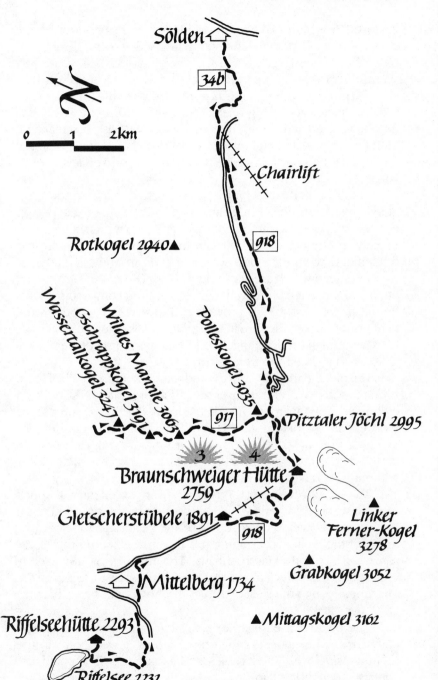

centered in Sölden. Make your way down from the pass towards the parking area but branch left about halfway down and head to the base of the Polleskogel. There's a very steep and loose but short scramble up a cabled track to a small pass. On the way up you see a sign warning that this climb is *nur für Geubte;* at the top is another warning, pictorial, that high-heeled shoes should not be worn! (You may be amazed at the amount of hardware that has been manhandled into impossibly high places, but it usually has some practical application. This one is just for entertainment, and a great success it is, too.)

At this point the real journey starts, with the path winding just below the first stretch of ridge and then roughly clinging to the top of it the whole way to the *Biwak* (bivouac). The walk takes approximately three and a half hours from this small saddle and it is fundamentally an extended scramble over an endless jumble of rocks, some of which are alarmingly loose. The route, for it cannot be described as a path, is well marked with red paint and presents no navigational problems providing the weather is good. Prominent points on the ridge are marked with tall wooden poles and the bivouac, a small bright orange module at the summit of the Wassertalkogel, is visible from time to time.

Despite the frequency of the red marks, keeping track of them requires some concentration, especially as precipitous drops lie on either side of the route in some places. The need for proper footwear is obvious in all this, both for foot protection and for gripping the rock over which you are clambering. You may be tempted to wear your training shoes because you have a day without a rucksack. This would be simply foolhardy.

The scenic rewards of this ridge walk are excellent, with much of the last two days' walk visible to the west by the time you reach the Wassertalkogel. You look down on the Pitztal and Mittelberg for much of the walk and, heading north, you can see up the Taschachtal as far as the Taschachhaus. The Riffelsee is also clearly visible, as is the waterfall by which you climbed yesterday. Even the Ölgruben Joch to the west of the Taschachhaus will be visible on a good day.

The bivouac itself is an extraordinary piece of mountain architecture: a hexagonal orange box on legs, guyed down to the mountainside with steel cables and looking as if it could not contain much more than a first aid kit. Its effect, however, is rather like Doctor Who's Tardis; it has the amazing ability to appear bigger inside than seems possible from the outside, for it contains no fewer than nine bunks, complete with mattresses and blankets, a table, a couple of gas camping stoves, emergency food supplies, water, plates and cutlery, even packs of cards, *and* a first aid kit. The visitors' book contains a photograph of the shell being lowered onto the summit by helicopter. A corrugated iron privy is perched precariously on a ledge a short distance away. The door of the bivouac is always unlocked, as it is obviously unwardened. It is used for more than just emergency accommodation, but the number of people staying overnight there is controlled from the Braunschweiger Hütte. Sitting on its wooden steps you look almost directly onto the Wildspitze, rising considerably above all else in the region. To its west rises the Taschachwand.

Allow three and a half hours to get back to the Braunschweiger Hütte from the bivouac. As your fatigue increases, your ability to stay upright on the treacherous rocks decreases. *Do not hurry.* Take particular care descending the short stretch on the side of the Polleskogel before reclimbing the Pitztaler Jöchl.

DAY 4

Braunschweiger Hütte (2759 m) to Sölden (1367 m) via Pitztaler Jöchl (2995 m)

Time: 3.5 hours
Distance: 10 kilometers (6.2 miles)
Viewpoints: Pitztaler Jöchl
Access: Road from Sölden

This is a half-day walk, mostly under easy conditions, to a valley with good communications to the outside world. Apart from the initial climb to the Pitztaler Jöchl, it is downhill all the way — a descent of some 1400 meters.

From the Braunschweiger, retrace yesterday's steps as far as the Pitztaler Jöchl, but head straight down from the pass to the parking area. A large restaurant lies at the bottom to your right, kept well supplied with skiers by a regular bus service from Sölden. Go to the eastern end of the parking area and find a track, still the E5 but apparently not much frequented. It runs along the side of the mountain and gradually down to the road, which should be visible all the time. Cross straight over the road and wind your way down to cross the river. Walk down for a couple of kilometers below and

Rhein-Pfalz Biwakschachtel — an emergency shelter (Richard Cox photo)

parallel to the road, on its southern side. The Kompass Wander-karte shows the E5 running just above the road on its north side, but the track below is quite obvious, so I suggest you take it. Further down the valley you will see the other track running parallel to the road and some way above it.

The track hits the road again after about 2 kilometers. Walk down the road for a short way, then turn left off it a short way above a large road toll station. The track leads down by a stream and past a new winding station for a chair lift. Here one is apparently offered two routes to Sölden: one, going straight down the hill, is marked *schwer* (difficult) on the signpost. The other goes gently downhill over a grassy track before plunging steeply into pine woods, zig-zagging all the way to Sölden. It crosses the road twice. This is a hard descent, but the constant jarring on your legs is alleviated somewhat by the soft ground underfoot. As you near Sölden, you pass a large church, and soon after walk on to the town's main street. There are many guest houses, restaurants, and hotels, all, of course, immaculately well kept.

Sölden is a tourist town. It exploits that potential to the full, but manages to do so with style and taste. No doubt the good people of Sölden are aware that visitors expect to see wooden-fronted chalets dotted neatly around a green valley beneath towering mountains, but the reasons for the preservation of such a scene are more than just pecuniary. Even the newest hotels are built in the traditional style: broad, gently sloping roofs with wide eaves overshadowing balconies that quite often run the whole width of the building; baskets of geraniums or some other vividly colored flowers hanging from the balcony—at regular intervals, of course; and everywhere much emphasis on wood. A glance at one of these places in the early stages of its construction shows the "woodenness" to be a veneer, but an attractive and well made one at least. The architecture of a place like Sölden, which is quite a typical valley town, has some element of the candy box about it, but it is also a real place, where people live and work.

If, after this short crossing of the Ötztaler Alps, you want to visit the Stubai Alps, you are well placed at Sölden to do so. Regular bus service goes north up the Ötztal. To follow the Stubai itinerary (Tour 5), you should travel as far as Längenfeld.

No "stilletto heels" en route to Rhein-Pfalz Biwakschachtel (Richard Cox photo)

~*TOUR 4*~

The Ötztaler Alps
Obergurgl to Vent

Route: *Obergurgl – Langtalereck Hütte –
Hochwilde Haus – Ramol Haus – Martin Busch Hütte –
Kreuzspitze – Similaun Hütte – Schöne Aussicht –
Im Hintern Eis – Hochjoch Hospiz – Brandenburger Haus –
Vernagt Hütte – Breslauer Hütte – Vent*

Lasting seven or eight days, this tour offers a more comprehensive look at the Ötztaler Alps. Starting at the well-known village of Obergurgl, south of Sölden, the route works its way west and south, touching on the Italian border. It then heads north into the icy wastes of the Weisskamm before turning east to finish at Vent.

The main point of communication is the Ötztal station on the main Inn Valley railway line. Post buses run from here to Obergurgl, your starting point, which is about one and a half hours to the south. Ötztal has a money exchange and a supermarket.

Maps: 1:25,000 Alpenvereinskarten: No. 30/1 Ötztaler Alpen, Gurgl; No. 30/2 Ötztaler Alpen, Weisskugel; No. 30/3 Ötztaler Alpen,

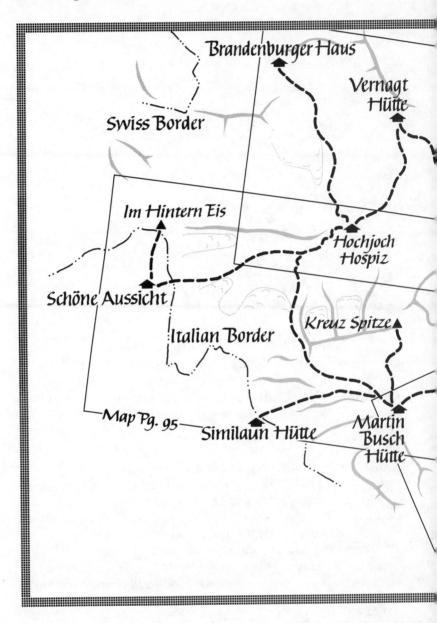

Brandenburger Haus

Vernagt Hütte

Swiss Border

Im Hintern Eis

Hochjoch Hospiz

Schöne Aussicht

Italian Border

Kreuz Spitze

Map Pg. 95

Similaun Hütte

Martin Busch Hütte

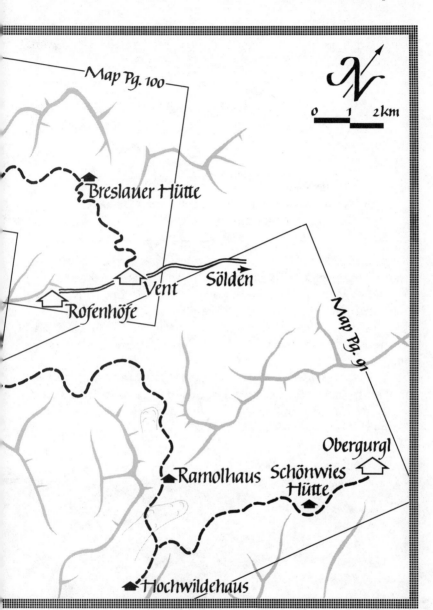

Map Pg. 100

0   1   2km

Breslauer Hütte

Vent   Sölden

Rofenhöfe

Map Pg. 91

Obergurgl

Ramolhaus   Schönwies Hütte

Hochwildehaus

Kaunergrat Geigenkamm. Note: You need maps with *Wegmark-ierung* (walking routes) rather than those marked with *Skirouten* (skiing routes).

DAY 1

Obergurgl (1927 m) to Ramol Haus (3006 m) via Langtalereck Hütte (2430 m) and Hochwilde Haus (2873 m)

> *Time:* 6 hours
> *Distance:* 14 kilometers (8.68 miles)
> *Viewpoints:* Hochwilde Haus, Ramol Haus
> *Access:* Obergurgl

Take route 922 out of Obergurgl. This easy walk can be made even easier by the use of a chair lift in Obergurgl. This saves you about 20 minutes walking time and about 120 meters of ascent. After about an hour you pass the privately owned Schönwies Hütte, which sells drinks. Next you pass Christian shrine and an old customs hut, and shortly after this you descend to the Langtalereck Hütte.

A *Materialseilbahn* (a cable car used by huts for hauling supplies up) connects the Langtalereck and Hochwilde huts; it can be used for transporting rucksacks if they are proving too heavy on the first day out.

Schalfkogel from path to Hochwilde Hütte (B. Swift photo)

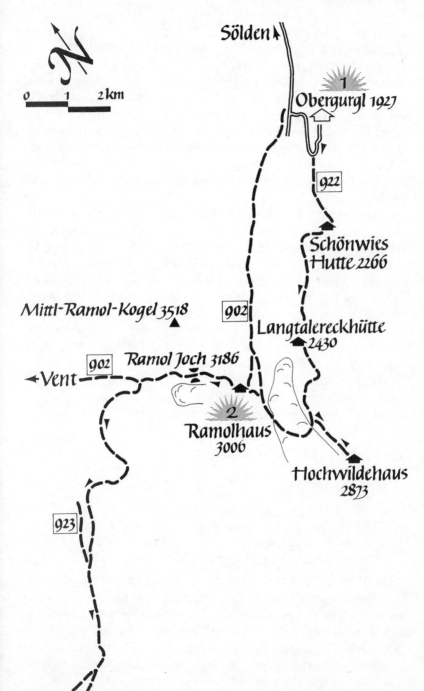

Below the Langtalereck Hütte, the path descends past a sober-
ing plaque to a guide who died going to someone's rescue. It then
crosses the stream from the Langtalerferner on a good bridge and
ascends to the shoulder of the Schwarze Spitze, climbing in short
zigzags. The remains of wire handholds are still partly attached to
the rocks. Around the corner, the path emerges on the lateral
moraine of the Gurgler Ferner. A small lake not marked on the
1:50,000 map is passed before the last rise to the Hochwilde Haus.
You are approaching brilliant snow scenery, and in good weather
you will need goggles to look at the Schalfkogel and other enticing
peaks around the glacier.

Heading for the Ramol Haus, retrace your steps back towards
the Langtalereck Hütte for 1.5 kilometers and turn left at the cairned
path that leads down to the Gurgler Ferner. The path drops down to
2560 meters on the west edge of the glacier, which is quite "dry"
and only a short walk across. Having crossed the glacier, you are
faced with a climb of 446 vertical meters in 1.5 kilometers. The
Ramol Haus hangs tantalizingly above you, but the climb is well
worth the effort, both for the views and for the hut's atmosphere.

The Ramol Haus has sinks for washing on the landings, but for
walkers who want a little more privacy, a jug and basin are provided
in the *Matratzenlager.* Although there are gaslights in the *Gaststube,* upstairs you will need a light in the evenings.

DAY 2

Ramol Haus (3006 m) to Martin Busch Hütte (2501 m) via the
Ramoljoch (3186 m)

Time: 5 hours
Distance: 11.25 kilometers (7 miles)
Viewpoints: Ramoljoch
Access: Vent

Take the path behind the hut to the Ramoljoch, which in normal
summer conditions takes half an hour to reach. The path across the
snow leads to a signpost pointing to the *Joch.* A short ladder helps
get you over the initial rock step, and from there the rocks are
waymarked to the pass so do not be put off by its appearance from
afar. Follow the path down over scree and a short section of glacier
onto the morainal heaps. Thirty minutes past the pass, the path

splits; one path goes down to Vent, but the one you want turns left towards the Niedertal. "Martin Busch" is written in red paint on a rock here, and more red paint marks send you across the stream and contouring over scree slopes. Presently you reach a pleasant grassy path from which you can spot the day's objective. On your left the sharp pinnacles of the west ridge of the Firmisanschneide pierce the sky. Amongst the rocks beside the path, marmots may be seen and heard.

You descend steeply to cross the Diembach above a waterfall; a smaller waterfall tumbling onto the path before this could provide a shower for the hardy. The path loses height rapidly and you approach the Niedertaler Ache. The bridge across this, which joins the main path from Vent to the Martin Busch Hütte, is a snow bridge which I am assured is permanent. (It is marked as a bridge on the map and is an exceptionally avalanche-prone spot in winter.) Not until the very last bend in this path do you see the hut.

Martin Busch Hütte is a substantial establishment that caters to large numbers. It has good facilities, including electricity. It took its present name in 1956 from a member of the Austrian Alpine Club who had done much to get it built. Previously it had been known as the Samoarhütte. Because of the large dining room and the potential problems for the staff, you pay as you would in any other restaurant, instead of running up a bill for the whole of your stay, as in many other huts.

DAY 3

Martin Busch Hütte (2501 m) to the Kreuzspitze (3457 m) and back

Time: 5 hours
Distance: 6 kilometers (3.72 miles)
Viewpoints: Kreuzspitze
Access: Vent

The Martin Busch Hütte is justly popular, being in such a strategic position and easily accessible from Vent, which is a two-and-a-half-hour climb away.

Having been on the summit of many Ötztal peaks, I can confirm that the Kreuzspitze remains one of the best views of all. It is exciting to sit on the summit identifying all the mountains as well as seeing the huts you are to visit. The Ortler, the Dolomites, the Stubai, the Silvretta, and beyond are all visible. This walk does, however, involve some scrambling up loose scree onto the summit ridge, and even in summer there occasionally may be one patch of unavoidable snow, for which, in descent, you might be happier to have an ice axe in your hand. Once on the ridge, keep to the rocks entirely. It is a steep ascent most of the way, with a little respite as you pass the remains of the old Brizzi Hütte, dating from 1865. An enormously solid cross stands on the summit as a memorial to Franz Senn, the vicar of Vent from 1860 to 1872; he did much to encourage mountaineering in the Ötztal and the Stubai and has had a hut in the Stubai Alps named after him. It is possible to see the Brandenburger Hütte from here, so keep looking, as its position is extraordinary.

DAY 4

Martin Busch Hütte (2501 m) to Similaun Hütte (3019 m) and back

Time: 3 hours
Distance: 9 kilometers (5.58 miles)
Viewpoints: Similaun Hütte
Access: Vent

From the Martin Busch Hütte, the path runs more or less parallel to the Niederjoch Bach and then rises onto the moraine above the glacier. It levels out as it crosses the snow and you reach the Similaun Hütte, the old frontier post, and a worn noticeboard announcing the border into Italy. Farther on, the Similaun Hütte is built on the edge of steep rocks that descend towards the Schnalstal of the Sudtirol. Its ramshackle appearance belies a cozy wood-lined interior; the red wine from the barrel provides a good excuse to stay awhile. You may even buy some wine for your water bottle and transport it for your evening meal back at the Martin Busch Hütte. Except in the enamel jugs in the rooms upstairs, water seems to be unavailable for public use. The toilets, although indoors, would in some respects have been better left outside. As the hut is privately run, the Alpine Club card does not bring the normal reduction for the overnight fee.

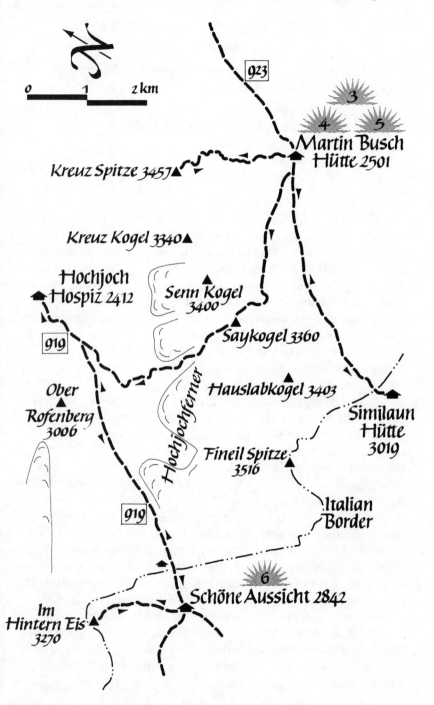

N

0   1   2 km

923

3

4   5

Martin Busch
Hütte 2501

Kreuz Spitze 3457▲

Kreuz Kogel 3340▲

Hochjoch
Hospiz 2412▲

Senn Kogel
3400▲

Saykogel 3360▲

919

Hochjochferner

Hauslabkogel 3403▲

Ober
Rofenberg
3006▲

Similaun
Hütte
3019▲

Fineil Spitze
3516▲

Italian
Border

919

6

Schöne Aussicht 2842▲

Im
Hintern Eis
3270▲

DAY 5

Martin Busch Hütte (2501 m) to Schöne Aussicht Hütte (Bella Vista) (2842 m) via the Saykogel (3360 m)

Time: 5 hours
Distance: 9 kilometers (5.58 miles)
Viewpoints: Saykogel
Access: Vent

Start up the path to the Similaun Hütte and after a few minutes branch right on the Saykogel path. Gaining height, wind your way between waymarked rocks, up to and along the east ridge, finally turning up the south ridge to gain the summit. This is almost as good a viewpoint as the Kreuzspitze but not quite. If you decide that the rocks and no more than a dozen steps on snow, immediately beyond the summit on the west ridge, are more than you wish to attempt — it looks much worse than it is — you can retrace your steps down the south ridge for about 150 meters and turn west on a path that runs below the summit on its south side. This rocky path then joins the west ridge route further on. You can, of course, bypass the summit entirely on this path.

After leaving the ridge the terrain is open boulder and scree slopes with an energetic stream tumbling its way down from the glacier to your left. You have a choice: either to descend on the marked path to point 2470 meters and join the path from the Hochjoch Hospiz to the Schöne Aussicht, losing height which must be regained, or to traverse left below the ice cliffs and then make for the "dry" snout of the Hochjochferner. Be sure to cross the stream as high as possible, at about the 2800-meter contour, then make your way rather tediously over fairly steep scree, dropping a little to cross the Hochjochferner at about the 2700-meter level. A short scramble up the scree on the other side will take you up onto the main path. It is perfectly safe to cross this short bit of glacier but it feels strange crunching your way over the ice with rivulets of water running underneath — a bit like treading on bowls of Rice Krispies.

Near an old toll post and some disused army huts you cross into Italy and soon after reach the Schöne Aussicht, where the view is good but not as spectacular as might be expected from the name, which means "beautiful outlook."

Chamois sidesteps a glacier. (Bob & Ira Spring photo)

The Schöne Aussicht Hütte is another private hut, so there is no reduction with an Alpine Club card, but the inclusive price for *Matratzenlager,* dinner, and breakfast was good value, payable in Austrian schillings or Italian lire. The dining rooms are run cafeteria-style, but the range of drinks and the *Apfelstrudel* help to compensate for lack of atmosphere. The hut caters to both summer and winter skiers. The communal wash basins had the unexpected luxury of slightly warm water, so you could save your laundry until you reach here. There is electricity both downstairs and upstairs.

DAY 6

Round trip from Schöne Aussicht (2842 m) to Im Hintern Eis (3270 m); then to Hochjoch Hospiz (2412 m)

Time: 5 hours
Distance: 9.5 kilometers (5.89 miles)
Viewpoints: Im Hintern Eis
Access: Rofenhöfe

It is well worth adding Im Hintern Eis to your itinerary for the unobstructed view of the magnificent Weisskugel as well as for the benefit of obtaining a better perspective of the area in general. The peak also affords a view immediately south that you cannot achieve elsewhere on this tour. The path goes up the hillside behind the Schöne Aussicht Hütte. It is an enjoyable stony track, especially near the summit. Looking at the Weisskugel you may be able to see little knots of people on the Hintereis Joch to the south of the summit, as they struggle up the snow and over the Bergschrund. From the summit back to the hut is probably less than an hour.

As you descend the path to the Hochjoch Hospiz, it is hard to imagine that this famous pass route was the cause of the death of Franz Senn's most respected friend, Granbichler, when they were caught in a snowstorm in November 1868. We must remember that their clothing and boots were not the lightweight, efficient materials of today, and that the effects of cold and wind on a person were not so well known. Granbichler had been responsible for a number of first ascents in the area and his death weighed heavily on Franz Senn. Senn had been one of the first members of the Austrian Alpine Club in 1862, and after this tragedy he and two friends founded the German Alpine Club in May 1869, in Munich. Franz Senn personally borrowed money for the building of a better track from Rofen over the Hochjoch to the Schnalstal.

You will notice a bridge over the stream coming from the Saykogel route and shortly afterwards, on the opposite hillside, are the ruins of the old Hochjoch Hospiz, first built in 1869 by the Rofenhöfe guide Benedikt Klotz on Franz Senn's initiative. It was twice destroyed by avalanches, once in 1876 and again in 1924.

Curious sheep often greet walkers in this region. (Bob & Ira Spring photo)

The last part of the walk looks like hard work: a series of zigzags to reach the Rofen Ache and a sharp ascent to the hut. Sometimes it is difficult to gauge how long this type of terrain will take, but from first viewing the hut once you are round the shoulder of the Arzbödele, you will probably need less than an hour to reach it.

In the dining room of the Hochjoch Hospiz there is no printed menu as in other huts, but the hut warden may give you a choice of pork or beef dishes; they are very tasty and served with rice and salad. For fifteen extra schillings here you can have a bed in a lovely little room containing a table, a large wooden bunk (you need an aluminum ladder with the upper bed to attain its heights), and a washstand supporting the usual bowl and jug. Strong cotton towels were provided. The hut has electricity on all floors and plenty of toilets on the first and ground floors.

DAY 7

Hochjoch Hospiz (2412 m) to Brandenburger Haus (3272 m)

Time: 2.5 hours
Distance: 5.9 kilometers (3.65 miles)
Viewpoints: Brandenburger Haus
Access: Rofenhöfe

Although this walk makes only a very short day, I have included it as it would be a pity to miss the Brandenburger Haus, one of the highest in the Eastern Alps. Once there it would be a shame not to spend the night — it was built on the end of a rock rib in the middle of a sea of snow and ice, where the crests of the waves are rock ridges rising from shallow troughs of snow. The sunsets can be a riveting display of quickly changing colors, after which you hurry inside, as the cold air makes itself felt at this altitude.

It should be emphasized that the glacier crossing here is much higher and altogether a more serious proposition than the rest of this route. This is especially true in bad weather, in which case only a roped party with crevasse rescue equipment and expertise should cross. Always check with the hut warden to be sure there are no hazards. I would advise doing the walk in the first half of the morning so that the snow is still crisp and the sun not too hot. If the weather is uncertain, do not attempt the walk as storms

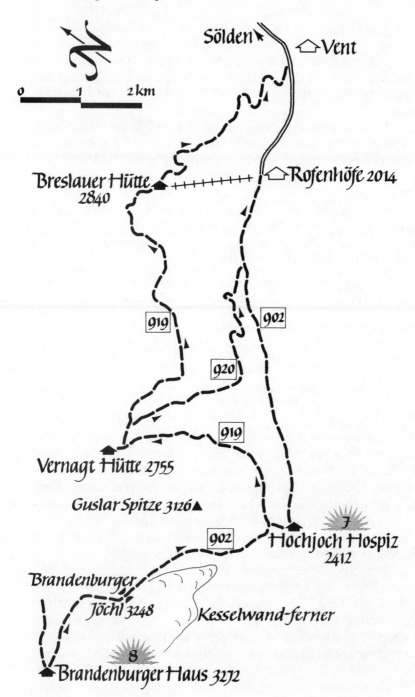

can arrive very quickly and once on the snow plateau, conditions could become as severe as in winter.

Follow the path behind the Hochjoch Hospiz, taking the left fork when the path divides. This is called the Delorette Weg. Hintereisferner to the southeast is like an open page in a geography book on terminal and lateral moraines. Higher up, on a narrow path on a steep hillside, you climb above the spectacular icefall of the Kesselwandferner. Once on the glacier, the way should be very straightforward.

Once at the Brandenburger, if the altitude has not taken too much out of you, scramble up the rocks and snow slope behind the hut onto the Dahmann Spitze, 3401 meters, and the highest point of the tour.

The Brandenburger Haus is quite a large hut designed by Richard Dahmann, after whom the peak behind the hut is named. The *Gaststube* gives an immediate impression of history with the old stove, its pipe leading up through the ceiling, and the gas lamps hanging over the tables. Around the walls hang well-mounted photographs picturing previous wardens and staff shoveling snow away from the entrance. Good-humored, hand-painted notices give the place a cared-for atmosphere. Unfortunately, the dining room accommodations do not match the bed numbers, so two or three sittings might be necessary if you hit a busy night.

Washing is limited to one communal trough and the toilets are self-flushing. Despite this, but not surprisingly, your night's stay costs a little more up here.

DAY 8

Brandenburger Haus (3272 m) to Vent (1896 m) via Hochjoch Hospiz path, Vernagt Hütte (2766 m) and either Breslauer Hütte (2840 m) or Rofenhöfe (2014 m)

> *Time:* 5 to 6 hours
> *Distance:* 18 to 20 kilometers (11.16 to 12.4 miles)
> *Viewpoints:* Vernagt Hütte
> *Access:* Vent

Today's walk can be terminated at Vernagt or Breslauer huts if desired.

Rofenhof, near journey's end for walkers from Obergurgl to Vent (Tyrolean National Tourist Office, Innsbruck, photo)

Retrace the route of the previous day to the divide in the path above the Hochjoch Hospiz. Do not descend to the hut, but take the eastward trail toward the Vernagt Hütte. Short stretches of the path require some concentration as the hillside is steep and the path narrow. The splash of the ever-present river and, if you are fortunate with the weather, the chirps of the grasshoppers will accompany you. A number of streams cross the route. Once round the shoulder of the Unter Rofenberg you will see the Vernagt Hütte not far away. It is in a strategic position at the junction of two moraines; both have paths on their ridges, providing a quick means of reaching the two glaciers, the Guslarferner and the Gross Vernagtferner. These glaciers now lie well up their valleys beyond the hut but they have joined and advanced very rapidly in the past. As late as 1848 the glacier filled the whole valley, preventing the waters of the Hintereis and the Hochjoch glaciers from escaping. A lake called the Rofensee formed, and caused great devastation when it overflowed. An Englishman I spoke to at the hut was revisiting after twenty years; he was surprised to see so much less of the Guslarferner from the hut, even in that period of time.

On the roof of the Vernagt Hütte is a bell, as at the Brandenburger. Historically, the bell had two uses: to guide people who might be making for the hut when it was misty, and for ringing on a Sunday when a guide and his friends would come up from the village and hold a service at the hut before climbing a mountain.

An effort has been made to maintain a homey atmosphere despite extensions to the hut. The *Gaststube* is wood-lined and copper lamp shades hang over each table. There are good facilities and the sleeping arrangements cater to nearly every size party, there being quite a warren of *Matratzenlager* and bedrooms.

From the Vernagt Hütte you can choose whether to descend to Vent via the Breslauer Hütte, so passing directly beneath the Wildspitze and with an opportunity to see the spectacular Rofenkarferner close to the hut, or more directly by the valley route via Rofenhöfe. I enjoyed this latter walk very much due to coming away from the barren glacial landscape towards the green pastures of the valley. Near Rofenhöfe in August, the heather is in bloom and the bilberries are plentiful. In Rofenhöfe, it is preferable to cross the River Rofe to continue to Vent on the southern side, rather than walk on the road.

The people of Rofenhöfe and Vent have been making a living from tourism for over 100 years. Their pasture space was always limited by the surrounding rock and glacier and so the mountaineering clergyman Franz Senn is said to have sought an alternative source of income for local people. In 1870, the Wildspitze was climbed by a tourist for the first time, led by several local guides, including Senn himself. So tourism and guiding started, and now many people of Vent run hotels, restaurants and shops. It is still a small village, though, and I think it has retained a certain charm, especially when you see families scything a steep hillside field. It is in the inner Alpine dry region, where the Weisskamm range, including the Wildspitze, keeps off north and west winds that carry rain.

From Vent, you can catch a bus to Sölden.

—Belinda Swift

ᗒᢩTOUR 5ᗒᢩ

The Stubai Alps

Route: *(Längenfeld) – Gries – Westfalen Haus –*
Franz Senn Hütte – Neue Regensburger Hütte –
Dresdner Hütte – Nürnberger Hütte – Stubaital

The Stubai Alps are the eastern neighbors of the Ötztal Alps, the two being separated by the Ötztal itself. They are quite heavily glaciated and contain some major peaks, including the Ruderhof Spitze (3474 meters), Schrankogel (3496 meters), and Zuckerhütl (3505 meters). The area is exceedingly well trodden and well "hutted," making many variations possible on the five-day route described here.

The region is bounded to the east by the Ötztal, which runs south from Innsbruck to the Italian border at Brenner, and to the south by the Italian border itself. However, even the southern end of the area is just a couple of hours' bus ride from Innsbruck. The Stubaital, the valley that runs into the heart of the region, is extremely well equipped for visitors. Access is from the Ötztal to the west or from various points in the Stubaital.

Map: Kompass Wanderkarte 1:50,000, No. 83, Stubaier Alpen Serleskamm.

Glacier seen en route to Nurnberger Hütte (Richard Cox photo)   105

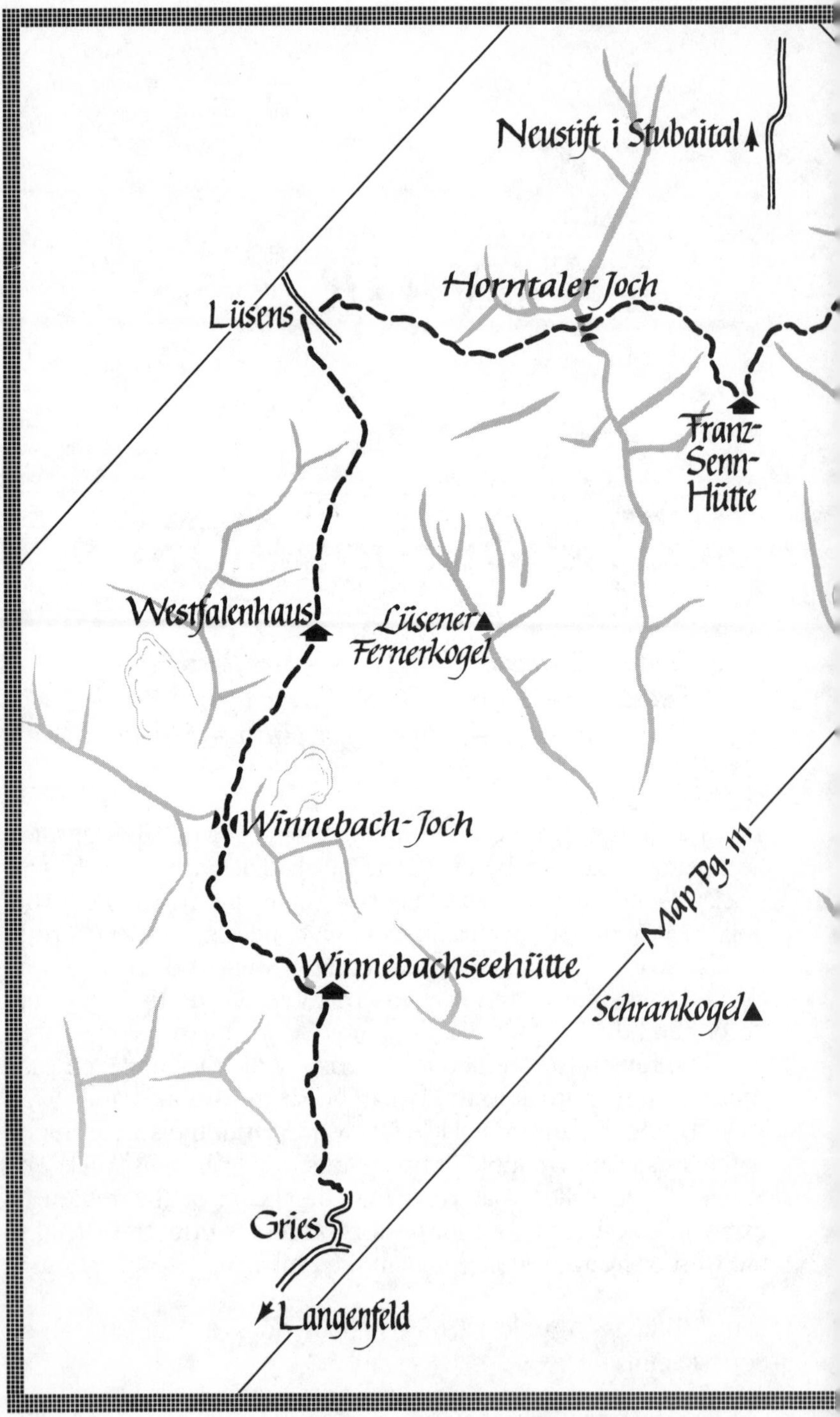

Neustift i Stubaital

Horntaler Joch

Lüsens

Franz-
Senn-
Hütte

Westfalenhaus

Lüsener
Fernerkogel

Winnebach-Joch

Map Pg. 111

Winnebachseehütte

Schrankogel

Gries

Langenfeld

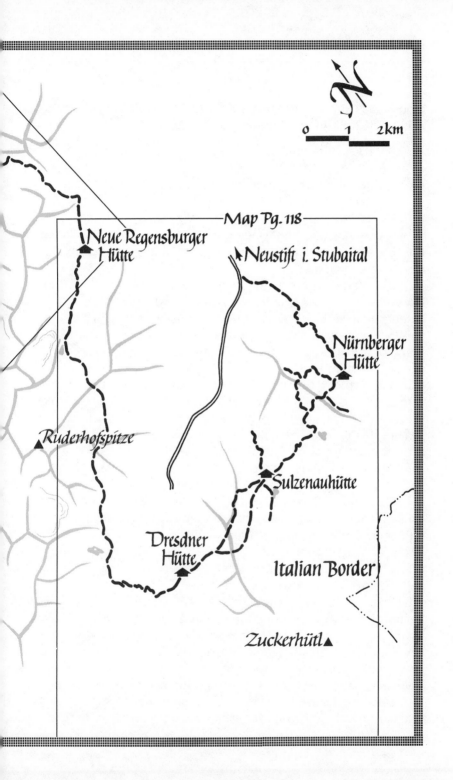

0   1   2km

Map Pg. 118

Neue Regensburger Hütte

Neustift i. Stubaital

Nürnberger Hütte

Ruderhofspitze

Sulzenauhütte

Dresdner Hütte

Italian Border

Zuckerhütl

DAY 1

Gries (1569 m) to Westfalen Haus (2273 m) via Winnebachsee Hütte (2362 m) and Winnebach-Joch (2788 m)

> *Time:* 6 hours
> *Distance:* 9 kilometers (5.58 miles)
> *Viewpoints:* Winnebachsee Hütte and Joch; Westfalen Haus
> *Access:* Längenfeld; Gries

A lot of climbing (over 1200 meters) is involved in today's walk, but it is not thrown at you all at once and there are some delightful resting places on the way.

To start the walk, take the minibus that runs from the Gasthof Edelweiss at Längenfeld to the village of Gries to the east. It should be emphasized that this is *not* Gries im Sellrain, which is also in the area. In Gries, walk up the main street to a sign on the left pointing up a paved road to the Winnebachsee Hütte and other places. The road leads to a small group of guesthouses above the main part of the village. It is from here that the lift carrying supplies to the hut runs; you will probably be able to put your packs on the cable cars to save the labor of lugging them up the hill to the hut. To arrange this, telephone the hut from the wind-up phone in the shed at the bottom. You will probably be told to leave your luggage in the shed, where it will be loaded onto the next run. There is a small charge for this service, which you pay at the hut.

Thus unencumbered, you will enjoy more the magnificent walk up the valley. The path climbs steeply up through woods and then more gradually up the mountains above the tree line. You get lovely views of the valley, of the mountains to the west, and of the cable cars carrying your rucksacks to the hut.

The Winnebachsee Hütte, which you should reach in one and a half to two hours, is untypically small and truly hutlike. It is beautifully situated opposite a waterfall that marks the end of the valley you have just been climbing, but is marred somewhat by a small, rather stagnant lake at one side of the hut. However, the grassy terrace in front of the hut affords excellent views of the waterfall and the mountains above and is a fine place for lunch.

Dragging yourself away from this, follow the Westfalen Haus sign at the back of the hut. Navigation is no problem, as there are

Langenfeld, starting place for Stubai tour (Tyrolean National Tourist Office, Innsbruck, photo)

many red paint marks all the way to the hut. Exercise extra care picking your way over the rocks higher up the valley.

The initial climb is a steady tramp over rocky, gently rising ground. It gets steeper and rockier as you go, and you should take time to admire the magnificent wide valley you are climbing. It eventually becomes a boulder field, where even the obviously considerable efforts of local mountain climbers to build a recognizable path have failed. The red paint marks are therefore very useful at this stage and they will guide you to the pass via a number of "false horizons" that deceive you into thinking you have completed the climb. When you finally reach the pass, it will probably be about an hour and a half after leaving the hut.

The initial descent from the pass is very loose and steep. The rest of the way to the Westfalen Haus is less treacherous, but is very rocky and may have some stretches of snow.

The Westfalen Haus, built in 1908 and modernized in 1970, has a quiet, "off-the-beaten-track" feel to it. Situated at the junction of valleys running south and west and with no immediate access to glaciers, it is in a less spectacular position than some of the Ötztaler huts, but its location has its own peace and beauty. Its southwest-facing terrace looks out onto the Hoher-Seebleskogel and can be a gloriously hot sun trap late on a summer's afternoon. The food here, due to the small size of the hut, is limited in choice, but perfectly adequate. The *Matratzenlager* is clad in gleaming pine, in the best tradition of a modernized hut interior, but seems rather cramped.

Isolated Westfalen Haus makes a good stopping point in the Stubai alps. (Tyrolean National Tourist Office, Innsbruck, photo)

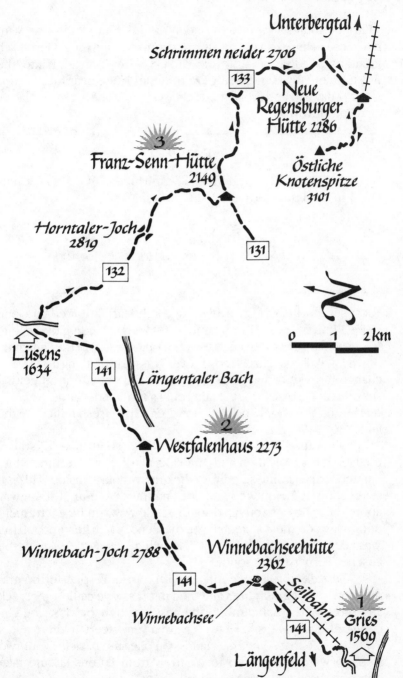

Unterbergtal

Schrimmen neider 2706

133

Neue
Regensburger
Hütte 2186

Östliche
Knotenspitze
3101

3

Franz-Senn-Hütte
2149

131

Horntaler-Joch
2819

132

N

0   1   2 km

Lüsens
1634

141

Längentaler Bach

2

Westfalenhaus 2273

Winnebach-Joch 2788

Winnebachseehütte
2362

141

Winnebachsee

Seilbahn

1

Gries
1569

141

Längenfeld

Alternate route: A two-day variation on this route leaves the Winnebachsee Hütte in a northerly direction, crossing the Zwieselbach Joch and heading north to the Guben Schweinfurter Hütte, the Finstertaler Hütte, and finally Dortmunder Hütte near Kuhtai. This is a two-day trip and is of a moderate standard. There are no glacier crossings involved.

DAY 2

Westfalen Haus (2273 m) to Franz Senn Hütte (2149 m) via Lüsens (1634 m) and the Horntaler Joch (2819 m)

Time: 8 hours
Distance: 11 kilometers (6.82 miles)
Viewpoints: The climb to Horntaler Joch
Access: Lüsens

Today's walk offers a spectacular but gentle start, followed by a long steep climb over the Horntaler Joch before descending to the hut.

The day starts with an easy walk along the side of the Längental down into Lüsens. This is mostly over grassland, making a welcome change from yesterday's relentless rock. Do not count on getting supplies at Lüsens, for it contains only a farm and a large *Gasthof/* restaurant. You should be able, however, to buy fresh milk from the farm.

Follow the signs to the Franz Senn Hütte south along the valley road for a short way, then find route 132, marked with red and white painted stripes going steeply up the grassy mountainside. This is a steep climb to begin with and does not moderate until some way above the valley. As you head south a little way, you have a tremendous view of the Langental you descended earlier and of the Westfalen Haus at the end of it. You will also see the edge of the Lüsener Ferner to the south.

The trek upwards continues with a brief respite in the gradient over a flat grassy area and then into a savage cauldron of rock and scree. The final climb to the pass can only be described — euphemistically — as hard work, with a very steep gradient and a loose surface that sometimes lands you one step back for your two steps forward. The climb to the pass from Lüsens should take between three and three and a half hours.

Franz-Senn Hütte (Bob & Ira Spring photo)

The pass itself is a mean ridge of rock that does not even allow much room for you to sit and eat lunch. However, your way down should be clear. It takes another hour and a half to the Franz Senn Hütte and you quickly forget about the severity of the climb as you amble down the mountain, mostly over pleasant grassy slopes and finally along the side of a valley to the hut. You will see the Oberiss Hütte first, in the valley at the lower end of the cable car line that serves the Franz Senn Hütte.

This hut is quite the opposite of the Westfalen Haus: it is a large, hotel-like place just a short walk up the mountain from a public road. It is old and woody inside and has a strange system for checking in, whereby you surrender your Alpine Club membership card upon arrival and then collect it later when an assistant takes your name, address, and money. This may be due to the fact that you are in a hut owned not by the German Alpenverein (which seems to run the majority of huts), but by its Austrian counterpart. Allegedly there are fewer Austrian huts because the Germans take their mountain pursuits more seriously than the Austrians and are not deterred by the fact that the huts are not in their own country. An Austrian once suggested to me that his people took a more casual attitude to their mountains. "If it is raining then *we* are not coming on the weekends to the mountains," he explained, implying that the Germans were not put off by such trifles as bad weather.

DAY 3

Franz Senn Hütte (2149 m) to Neue Regensburger Hütte (2286 m), then a climb of the Östliche Knotenspitze

Time: 3-1/2 hours to the hut
Distance: 6 kilometers (3.72 miles)
Viewpoints: Neue Regensburger Hütte
Access: Oberiss Hütte

It is just a morning's walk to the hut: a steady tramp up to the pass and then a steeper descent, for part of the way, to the hut, which you should reach in time for lunch. In the afternoon you can climb the Östliche Knotenspitze or relax around the hut.

The path leading south from the Franz-Senn winds slowly up the mountain, climbing gradually and then more steeply as it crosses scree. The final approach to the pass, little more than a knife edge of rock, is a fine sweep across the side of the valley. Overall, the path has been well engineered and well marked. The initial descent, as from many a pass, is steep and loose, but it levels out to give way to a pleasant piece of contouring the rest of the way to the hut, with the hut in sight for most of the final stretch.

Regensburger Hütte (J. Soutar photo)

The hut is remarkable only in that it has free hot showers, but this is enough of a rarity to boost its overall rating. It also has a very efficient *Trockenraum* (drying room) and a nice line in cakes. Outside is a noisy stream, which in the summer of 1985 was home to a pair of dippers. This extraordinary bird, seen in Britain mostly around waterways in the more mountainous western half of the country, lives perilously close to fast flowing water and seems in constant danger of being swept away. It can be seen hopping around on rocks and in muddy crevices on the very edge of the water and attracts attention by its swift, direct flight low over the water. Most surprisingly, it also swims underwater for short distances. Its portly shape and cocked tail make it look like an oversized wren, but its predominantly dark brown coloring is quite different from the smaller bird and it has a large white "bib" under its chin.

The climb to the Östliche Knotenspitze is a four-hour round trip, so you should start by 3:00 at the latest if you want to be back comfortably in time for dinner and before nightfall. You get fine views of glaciers to the northwest. The way up is clearly signposted from the hut and is a steep climb, initially over grassy mountainside.

DAY 4

Neue Regensburger Hütte (2286 m) to Dresdner Hütte (2302 m)
via Grawagrubennieder (2880 m) and the Mutterberger See

Time: 6 hours
Distance: 12 kilometers (7.44 miles)
Viewpoints: The first pass and much of the route
overlooking the Mutterbergtal
Access: Falbeson

This looks a dauntingly long way on the map, but it is easily done in
a day and contains only one major climb. Much of the route roughly
contours along the side of the Mutterbergtal, making a welcome
change from the up- and-over routine of previous days.

Walk up the apparently dead-end valley that lies behind the
Neue Regensburger Hütte and head for the lowest point in the
encircling mountains. The way is assiduously marked with red
paint. You will have to cross a small stretch of glacier at the foot of
the final climb to the pass and then up a fairly large snowfield. You
should have no problem crossing the glacier and there will probably be a line of steps kicked into the snow that forms perhaps half
the climb. Be warned that the rocks above this snow line are loose,
so you should exercise great caution both above and below it.

The view from the top should be, weather permitting, one of
the best you have had. Look across the Mutterbergtal to the Grosser
Trögler and the Maierspitze in the foreground and behind them to
large expanses of glacier overlooked by the major peaks of the
Aperer Pfaff (3351 meters), Zuckerhütl (3505 meters) and further
east the Wilder Freiger (3419 meters), the last forming part of the
Italian border.

Descend steeply at first and then contour down across the
scree and onto some grassland. Pass the Mutterberger See; from
this area you should be able to see the building at Mutterbergalm at
the bottom of the cable car run up to the Dresdner Hütte. The final
climb of the day is a short, sharp trek up the side of the Egesengrat,
after which it is just a short hop to the hut itself.

The Dresdner Hütte seems to have given up any pretensions
of being a mountain hut and has become a sort of down-market

Siegerland Hütte (Alison Wright photo)

hotel and staging post for skiers and trippers on their way from the valley to the glaciers above. It has bare rooms with bunks instead of the traditional wooden *Matratzenlager* and its *Gaststube* is scarred with a stainless steel self-service system reminiscent of a motorway service station. It does, however, have hot showers (for which you have to pay), and this redeems it somewhat. Its other redeeming feature is its proximity to the Zuckerhütl (3505 meters), the highest peak in the Stubai and one of the major peaks in the mountain ridge that marks the Austrian-Italian border. The peak is not recommended for inexperienced trekkers, although experienced parties may wish to attempt it in good weather.

DAY 5

Dresdner Hütte (2302 m) to Nürnberger Hütte (2280 m) via Peii Joch (2676 m), Sulzenau Hütte (2191 m) and Niederl Joch (2627 m)

> *Time:* 5 hours
> *Distance:* 7 kilometers (4.34 miles)
> *Viewpoints:* Peii Joch, Niederl Joch
> *Access:* Mutterbergtal (cable car to Dresdner Hütte)

This is a very satisfying day's walk — or not much more than half a day if you want to hurry. It does not involve a great variation in height and has a hut at about halfway where you can take lunch. The

Neue Regensburger Hütte 2286

Neustift, Fulpmes

Besuchalm 1600

138

134

Nürnberger Hütte 2280

Falbesoner See

Grawagruben-nieder 2880

Maierspitze 2781

Niederl Joch 2627

Gamsspitz 3100

Schafspitz 2760

Grünau See

Sulzenauhütte 2191

Grosser Trögler 2901

135

102

Mutterberger See

Peii Joch 2676

Dresdner Hütte 2302

5   6

Zuckerhütl 3505

Egesengrat

Mutterbergtal

0   1   2 km

length of the walk also allows time for a descent to the valley below the Nürnberger Hütte. You can catch buses at the end of the track from the Nürnberger to Innsbruck and points in the Stubaital.

From the door of the Dresdner, walk down the hill past the hideous cable car station with its endless stream of little red boxes going in and out and head up the side of the Grosser Trögler. Do not underestimate this climb — it involves an ascent of nearly 400 meters and much of it is steep and loose underfoot. A short way up is an alternative route to the Sulzenau Hütte via the summit of the Grosser Trögler. If you are not taking this, carry on up the well-marked route to the Peii Joch, where you will find a vast number of stone cairns that look as if someone has been running a course in dry stone construction. More impressive is the view of the Sulzenauferner, its great linear crevasses stretching across the mountain just below you.

The rest of the way to the Sulzenau Hütte is a rocky walk along the side of the Grosser Trögler, with one section over a gully that involves shuffling along a bridge made only of two steep pipes. A hand cable is comfortingly set into the rock.

The Sulzenau Hütte is well situated for a descent to the valley if your schedule demands it, but it would be a shame to miss the final stretch of the day's walk to the Nürnberger Hütte, which takes two

Dresdner Hütte with Schaufelspitze behind (Alison Wright photo)

Above the Nurnberger Hütte (Richard Cox photo)

and a half to three hours. If the Sulzenau is serving *Apfelstrudel,* be sure to try some before leaving — it was absolutely the best of our trip.

The route from the Sulzenau climbs, crosses a small river valley, and then runs parallel to and above the Grünau See (Green

Lake) for some way before arriving there. This small, inappropriately named lake is actually a vivid blue and contrasts brilliantly with the white of the glacier above.

Turn sharply and steeply left here and wind up a grassy mountainside to a small upper valley containing a shallow little lake and the turnoff to the Maierspitze. This is an alternative route to the Nürnberger Hütte and is, the sign tells you, *nur für Geubte.*

The final climb to the pass, whose crucifix you have been able to see for some time, is short and very steep with some cabled sections. From the top you have the unusual advantage of being able to see both the hut you have come from and the one you are going to. The Nürnberger appears comfortingly close in the midst of a landscape of rock directly below. The way down is well trodden but slow and hazardous in places and will take about an hour.

The Nürnberger Hütte, a solid, imposing stone building that blends in beautifully with its rocky surroundings, has a huge rock wall above it, presumably to protect against falls of rock or snow. The hut is well-situated for a climb of the Wilder Freiger. You may wish to stay overnight at the Nürnberger, but if not, it will take one and a half to two hours to get down to the valley from here. A large, well-trodden path takes you down to Besuchalm and then to the Stubaital. At various points in this descent, you will realize the enormous amount of work that has gone into building the path: large quantities of stone have been painstakingly stacked — no doubt by hand — to make a well-engineered trackway.

From Besuchalm, where refreshments are available, it is a steady tramp down the car-sized but unmade track to the main road. When you can see the road through the trees below, look for a small track going off to the left. This will take you by a more direct route to the road and the bus stop than the main track, which winds down the hill in a very leisurely manner.

The bus for Innsbruck and towns in the Stubaital leaves from the parking area at the bottom of the track.

∽*TOUR 6*∽

The Zillertal
High Route

Route: *Brenner – Landshuter Hütte – Olperer Hütte –*
Furtschagl Haus – Berliner Hütte – (Am Horn) –
Greizer Hütte – (Grosser Löffler) – Kasseler Hütte –
Edel Hütte – (Ahorn Spitze) – Mayrhofen

The Zillertaler Alps are one of the best known of Austria's Alpine ranges and are used extensively by walkers, climbers, and skiers. The range runs roughly northeast to southwest and lies to the southeast of Innsbruck. It is bounded to the west by the Eisacktal, leading south to Italy, and to the east by the lofty peaks of the Venediger Gruppe. To the north, the range is approached by the Zillertal, leading south from the Inn Valley and rising at Mayrhofen, a major ski resort and the jumping-off point for many Zillertal expeditions. The major peaks of the Zillertal include the Grosser Möseler (3478 meters), the Hochfeiler (3510 meters), and the Schwarzenstein (3368 meters).

The range is heavily glaciated, but some peaks are accessible to walkers with no technical expertise, providing they are prepared for some scrambling.

Mörchenscharte, the pass between Greizer Hütte and Berliner Hütte
(Art Farash photo)

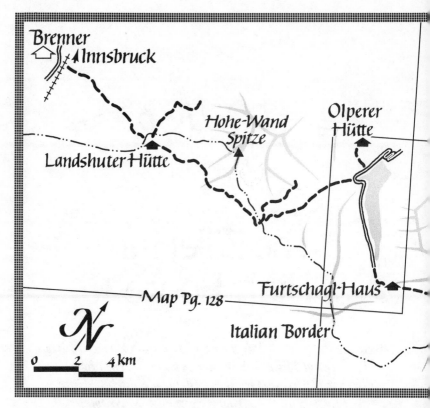

The walk described here lasts between seven and ten days and is along mostly well-graded and carefully waymarked paths that wend their way through magnificent mountain scenery. Most of the tour follows the Central Alps Way (Zentralalpenweg), which runs between the Pyrenees and eastern Austria.

Walkers are advised to carry an *ice axe* for this route. It will provide security for any isolated snow patches and can also be used as a walking stick. The walking experience needed for this route will vary according to weather conditions, since the route itself should not present any problems. If the weather has been warm there should be little or no snow left on the paths, but a sudden snowfall and freezing temperatures could turn some of the passes into dangerous places requiring some experience of severe conditions. Under such conditions, less experienced walkers are advised to retreat to the nearest valley or stay another night in the nearest hut in the hope of better weather the next day. The only place on

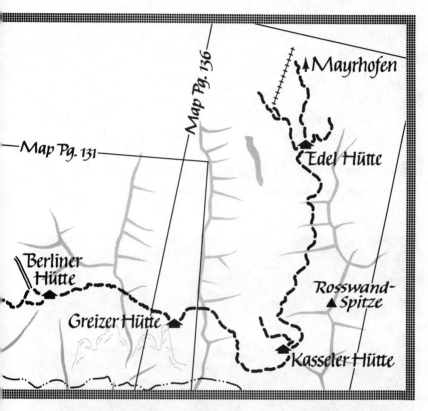

this route with permanent snow is the Mörchenscharte and if you are apprehensive about this a detour is possible (see Day 6).

This route's eastward progress is punctuated by three summit climbs, each of which will take the best part of a day and involve staying an extra night at the appropriate hut. A guide or climbing experience will be needed for the Grosser Löffler but not for the other two suggested climbs. Omitting the climbs will bring the overall tour down to about a week.

The route starts from Brenner, which is on the Italian border south of Innsbruck and easily reached by train from there. You head east to Landshuter Hütte and Pfitscherjoch Haus, then turn north to the Olperer Hütte near the lake known as the Schlegeisspeicher. From there the route runs by the lake, going southeast to the Furtschagl Haus where it resumes its easterly direction, visiting the Berliner, Greizer, and Kasseler huts. At the Kasseler Hütte, the tour turns north again, beginning the approach to Mayrhofen. A night is spent at the Edel Hütte with the option of a half-day climb of the nearby Ahorn Spitze before making the final descent to Mayrhofen.

Alternate route: A two-day variation on this route can be made by starting at Hintertux and heading south to the Tuxerjoch Haus, Kleegruben Scharte, Geraer Hütte, and Alpeiner Scharte, to join the Zillertal High Route at the Schlegeisspeicher on Day 2.

The paths from the valleys to the huts are always well maintained — they are used by tourists going to the huts for lunch and

Schlegeisspeicher, on the way to Olperer Hütte (Tyrolean National Tourist Office, Innsbruck, photo)

the wardens like to encourage such visitors. However, walkers who go beyond the huts will also find mostly clear and well-marked paths.

All the huts on the route are owned by the German Alpine Club. At some huts, guides are available for those wishing to climb nearby peaks covered by snow or ice. This is an ideal way to gain Alpine experience and to add some extra excitement to a walking holiday. The guides take the easiest routes up and only stamina is required to get to the top. Inquiries should be made at huts on arrival.

Maps: The 1:25,000 series published by the Austrian Alpine Club (OAV) provides the greatest detail of the maps generally available. Those needed are: Zillertaler Alpen West, 35/1 and 35/2, Mittl. Alternatives are the Freytag and Berndt 1:50,000 series, Nos. 241, Innsbruck and Brenner; and 152, Mayrhofen and Zillertal.

DAY 1

Brennersee Halt (1305 m) to Landshuter Hütte (2713 m)

> *Time:* 4 hours
> *Distance:* 7 kilometers (4.34 miles)
> *Viewpoints:* Kraxentrager (views of Venntal,
> Pfitschertal, Dolomites)
> *Access:* There is regular train service over the Brenner Pass from Innsbruck. You should get off at Brennersee Halt. A short distance away, at the top of the pass, are a few shops where you can buy supplies.

The path to the Landshuter Hütte, which sits on a pass, starts a few minutes from Brennersee Halt and is numbered either 531 or 528, depending on which map you have. It runs east up the Venntal, starting as a road and becoming a track. About 1.6 kilometers from the hut, the path turns left and climbs through meadows, flowers, and trees to the pass, which is contrastingly desolate. Above the pass and about one hour's scramble away is the Kraxentrager (2998 meters), from whose peak you can see part of tomorrow's route. You should also be able to see down into the Pfitschertal and south as far as the Dolomites.

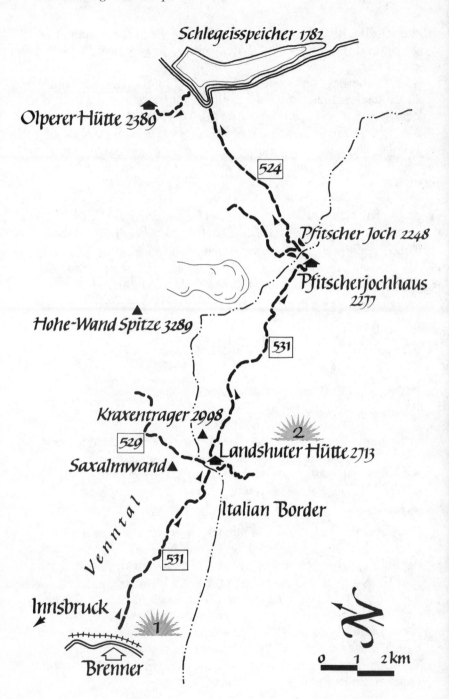

Schlegeisspeicher 1782

Olperer Hütte 2389

524

Pfitscher Joch 2248

Pfitscherjochhaus
2277

Hohe-Wand Spitze 3289

531

Kraxentrager 2098

2

529

Landshuter Hütte 2713

Saxalmwand

Italian Border

V e n n t a l

531

1

Innsbruck

Brenner

N

0   1   2 km

DAY 2

Landshuter Hütte (2713 m) to Olperer Hütte (2389 m) via Pfitscher Joch (2248 m) and Schlegeisspeicher (1782 m)

> *Time:* 6.5 hours
> *Distance:* 14 kilometers (8.68 miles)
> *Viewpoints:* Olperer Hütte
> *Access:* The road to Pfitscher Joch. Alternatively, you can take the bus that runs from Mayrhofen to the Schlegeisspeicher dam.

Leaving the Landshuter Hütte, path 531 is now called the Landshuter Hohenweg and it contours east to the Pfitscher Joch. This pass, on the Italian border, takes about three hours to reach. Refreshments are available at the Pfitscherjoch Haus, a short way above the pass.

Turning north here, route 531 becomes 524 and descends to the Schlegeisspeicher, which takes about two hours to reach. This lake is quite an attraction and the area is likely to be busy with tourists. It is at this point that the route joins the Zentralalpenweg.

Enjoying a toast with an alpine farmer (Tyrolean National Tourist Office, Mayrhofen, photo)

(The Zentralalpenweg, which runs from Feldkirch in the west of the country to Hainburg, Austria's easternmost town, is one of the most spectacular and difficult trails in the Alps. It measures 1200 kilometers, takes forty to fifty days to walk, and much of it is for experienced mountain walkers only.)

Turning left at the reservoir, walk along the road to the point at which path 502 leads to the Olperer Hütte. Climb the steep Riepenbach Gorge until it crosses the Riepenbach itself, then follow the zigzag path to the hut. This should take about one and a half hours.

The Olperer Hütte is perched high above the Schlegeisspeicher and offers very good views of the reservoir and the snowy peaks of the Zillertal range.

DAY 3

Olperer Hütte (2389 m) to Furtschagl Haus (2295 m) via Schlegeisspeicher (1800 m)

> *Time:* 3.5 hours
> *Distance:* 9 kilometers (5.58 miles)
> *Viewpoints:* Furtschagl Haus
> *Access:* The road from Mayrhofen to the Schlegeisspeicher.

Descend path 502 to the dam and turn right to walk along the track beside the water. The track continues to the goods lift for the Furtschagl Haus and then becomes a steep path up to the hut. Sometimes it is possible to put rucksacks and other luggage on goods lifts, but telephone from the lift to ask first. There may be a charge for this service.

From the Furtschagl Haus terrace, there are superb views of the glaciers and peaks to the south, including the Hochfeiler (3510 meters), the highest in the Zillertal Alps. Its sheer north face is particularly impressive. The path north from the hut towards the Grosse Greiner leads in half an hour to an interesting rock crystal outcrop.

You may be able to hire a guide from the hut to take you up the Grosser Möseler, a relatively easy peak and well worth the effort. This is an eight-hour round trip, so you will need to stay a second night at the Furtschagl Haus if you are going to do it.

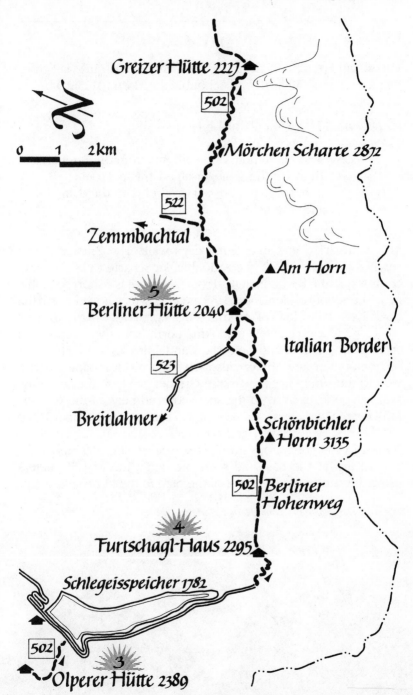

Greizer Hütte 2227

502

Mörchen Scharte 2872

522

Zemmbachtal

▲Am Horn

5
Berliner Hütte 2040

Italian Border

523

Breitlahner

Schönbichler
▲Horn 3135

502 Berliner
Hohenweg

4
Furtschagl-Haus 2295

Schlegeisspeicher 1782

502

3
Olperer Hütte 2389

DAY 4

Furtschagl Haus (2295 m) to Berliner Hütte (2040 m) via Schön-bichler-Scharte (3081 m) and Schönbichler Horn (3135 m)

Time: 5 hours
Distance: 7 kilometers (4.34 miles)
Viewpoints: Schonbichler Horn
Access: Walk three hours via path 523 from the Breitlahner Hütte on the Schlegeisalpenstrasse. From here there is a bus service between the dam and Mayrhofen.

This is a varied and interesting day's walk. The Zillertal Route reaches its highest pass, the Schönbichler-Scharte (3081 meters), on its way to the Berliner Hütte. From the pass it is a short scramble up to the Schönbichler Horn (3135 meters), which is well worth the diversion for the views of the knife-edge north ridge of the Grosser Möseler and the Hochfeiler. Looking north from the summit, you can see the Olperer and Gefrorne Wand Spitze as well as the next section of the route. You can also see a sharp ridge leading north-west to the summit of the Grosse Greiner, while to the south the same ridge leads away to the snow-covered peak of the Grosser Möseler (3478 meters). To the east you can see the Berliner Hütte and beyond; to the west and far below is the Furtschagl Haus, backed by the precipitous sides of the Hochsteller (3097 meters).

Return to the pass and scramble down the first 50 meters using the fixed ropes; the rest of the path to the hut is less steep.

Grosser-Moseler, seen from Schonbichlerhorn (Art Farash photo)

A warm September day on the Schonbichlerhorn (Art Farash photo)

The Berliner Hütte was once the hunting lodge of the Austrian emperor Franz Josef, and some of its grandeur remains in the form of high ceilings and the chandeliers in the dining hall. In its modern form as a mountain hut, it sleeps about fifty people. As it is so comfortable and efficiently run, it is worth staying two nights and using the extra day for rest and exploration. It is the lowest hut

On the Hornkees glacier, near Berliner Hütte (Art Farash photo)

on this route, and the area is very attractive with streams and meadows nearby.

Alternatively, you may stay at the privately owned Alpenrose Hütte (1875 meters), just below the Berliner.

DAY 5

Berliner Hütte (2040 m) to climb the Am Horn (2647 m)

Time: 4 hours round trip
Distance: 5 kilometers (3.1 miles)
Viewpoints: Am Horn
Access: Breitlahner; Zemmbachtal

The path to the Am Horn is also used to approach the Berliner Spitze and is therefore easy to find and well used. When you are below the Am Horn, turn left and climb steeply to the summit on an obvious path.

The climb to the Am Horn gives good views of the peaks and glaciers of the four Berlinerspitzen. It may also be possible to hire a guide for a climb to the highest of them, the Berlinerspitze. It is a seven-hour round trip.

Berliner Hütte (Tyrolean National Tourist Office, Innsbruck, photo)

DAY 6

Berliner Hütte (2040 m) to Greizer Hütte (2227 m) via Mörchenscharte (2957 m) and Floiten Valley (1834 m)

Time: 5 hours
Distance: 8 kilometers (4.96 miles)
Viewpoints: Mörchenscharte; Greizer Hütte
Access: Zemmbachtal

There are considerable height differences on this part of the Zentralalpenweg; the route descends over 1000 meters, from the top of the Mörchenscharte down to the head of the Floiten Valley.

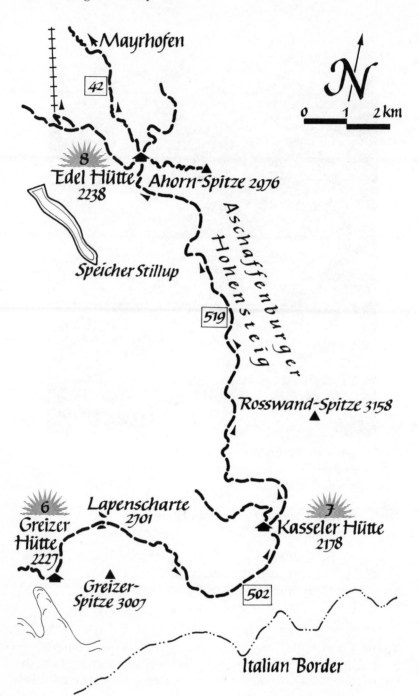

Mayrhofen

42

N

0   1   2 km

8

Edel Hütte
2238

Ahorn-Spitze 2976

Aschaffenburger Hohensteig

Speicher Stillup

519

Rosswand-Spitze 3158

6

Greizer
Hütte
2227

Lapenscharte
2701

Greizer-
Spitze 3007

7

Kasseler Hütte
2178

502

Italian Border

The gradients are easy as far as the Schwarzsee (2472 meters), a much-photographed beauty spot, but after this most of the day is spent on steep ground. Follow path 502 all day.

You will find permanent snow on the east side of the Mörchenscharte and care is needed here to negotiate the steep slopes. The route leaves the gully after a while and continues more easily down on the left side before entering the gorge near the bottom, where you may find more snow. There are many Alpine flowers to be seen here, including the famous edelweiss. After you cross the stream at 1834 m, the path zigzags up to the Greizer Hütte. From the hut you can look up to the Mörchenscharte and see the whole of the route down. It's a spectacular sight!

Alternate route: If you do not wish to tackle the Mörchenscharte, leave the route at the Berliner Hütte and take path 523 down the Zemmgrund, or walk as far as the Schwarzsee and divert onto path 522 through the Güggl Valley. Both these paths lead to the Dornasberger Tal road, which has bus service to Mayrhofen.

Early morning fog in the Floitengrund valley, north of Greizer Hütte. (Art Farash photo)

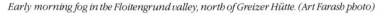

DAY 7

Greizer Hütte (2227 m) to Kasseler Hütte (2178 m) via Lapenscharte (2700 m)

Time: 4 hours
Distance: 8 kilometers (4.96 miles)
Viewpoints: Lapenscharte
Access: Stillup Grund (valley)

Follow path 502 all day, crossing many streams, some of which run over slabs of rock where wooden posts have been installed as an aid to walkers. The Kasseler Hütte can be seen from the Lapenscharte, across the head of the Stillup Valley. After crossing the pass, most of this route is on a fine contour path that leads to the hut.

Alternatively, if a guide can be hired, you can spend a day climbing the Grosser Löffler, and stay a second night at the Greizer Hütte. It is a seven-hour round trip.

DAY 8

Kasseler Hütte (2178 m) to Edel Hütte (2238 m)

Time: 8 hours via the high route; 6 hours via the valley
Distance: 12 kilometers (7.44 miles) via the high route;
15 kilometers (9.3 miles) via the valley
Viewpoints: Much of the Aschaffenburger Hohensteig
Access: From Mayrhofen via the Ahornbahn cable car

Here the route diverts from the Zentralalpenweg to follow the Aschaffenburger Hohensteig 519.

Given suitable conditions, this high route from the Kasseler to the Edel Hütte is highly recommended. The Aschaffenburger Weg takes a contouring line for most of its way between the two huts, giving good views of the Stillup Valley and its many waterfalls. However, you should *not* attempt this if the ground is wet: the steep, grassy slopes are extremely dangerous and the valley road is a safer alternative.

Kasseler Hütte (Art Farash photo)

The valley route goes steeply down to the Stillup Valley, followed by a long road walk to the lake and dam. There is a restaurant at the dam (1100 meters). From there, path 514 climbs to the top of the Ahornbahn cable car (1907 meters) and then continues at a more moderate gradient to the Edel Hütte.

The Edel Hütte is used mainly as a refreshment stop for day visitors. Very few people stay overnight and the atmosphere is quite different from that at other huts on this route which are frequented by walkers and climbers.

DAY 9

Edel Hütte (2238 m) to Ahorn-Spitze (2976 m) and back

> *Time:* 4 hours round trip
> *Distance:* 4 kilometers (2.48 miles)
> *Viewpoints:* Ahorn-Spitze
> *Access:* From Mayrhofen via the Ahornbahn cable car
> and path 514 to the Edel Hütte

The Ahorn-Spitze makes a fitting climax to this part of the Zillertal route, and should be easily reached in two hours, with a scramble at the top. This pinnacle stands apart from other nearby peaks and ridges, and is a fine viewpoint. You can see north right down the Zillertal, with Mayrhofen in the bottom of the valley, and south to the Grosser Löffler.

Train service connects Mayrhofen with the outside world. (Tyrolean National Tourist Office, Mayrhofen, photo)

DAY 10

Edel Hütte (2238 m) to Mayrhofen (633 m)

Time: 2.5 hours
Distance: 6 kilometers (3.72 miles)
Viewpoints: Ahornbahn cable car
Access: The Ahornbahn cable car

Take the path to the top of the Ahornbahn cable car, and enjoy a pleasant ride down to Mayrhofen. Alternatively, take path 42 down via the Alpenrose. Mayrhofen is a small town catering to a year-round tourist trade and is a good place for shopping and easing yourself back into the world below the Alps.

There is regular train service on the narrow gauge track from Mayrhofen to Jembach, sometimes using a steam engine. At Jembach it meets the mainline services to Innsbruck, Munich, Salzburg, and other major centers.

— Margaret Stickland and Bob Poore

TOUR 7

The Karwendel

Route: *Scharnitz – Brunnenstein Hütte – Hochland Hütte –*
Karwendelhaus – Round-trip to Birkkarspitze –
Lamsenjoch Hütte – Schwaz

Perhaps the most remarkable things about Innsbruck are the
mountains that surround it. They bear down on the city, hanging
hugely at the end of seemingly every street and dominating what is
otherwise a rather ordinary provincial center. To the north, these
mountains are the Karwendelgebirge, a range not distinguished by
major peaks, glaciers, or glamorous ski resorts, but having a particular beauty, plenty of huts and footpaths, and a consequent
magnetism for walkers.

The Karwendel consists of four main mountain ridges directly
to the north of Innsbruck. These ridges run east-west and have
valleys that drain into the River Isar at Scharnitz. The area has a
good network of marked paths, including the European long-
distance footpath E4. Due to the area's topography it is much easier
to walk west-east than north-south and it is possible to walk across
the Karwendel keeping in the valleys most of the time and so
avoiding any serious climbs.

For first-time Alpinists feeling a little trepidation, the Karwendel is a good bet: it will be relatively undemanding physically while

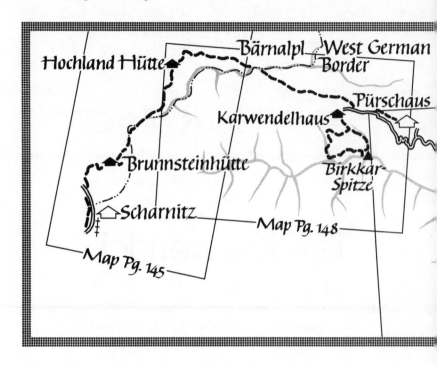

providing everything you could wish for in glorious Alpine scenery.

The classic Karwendel west-east route follows the valleys from Scharnitz to Pertisau. The route here diverges somewhat from that, covering a mixture of valley, ridge, and pass to take in a variety of

High-altitude rest stop on the Karwendel tour (Tyrolean National Tourist Office, Innsbruck, photo)

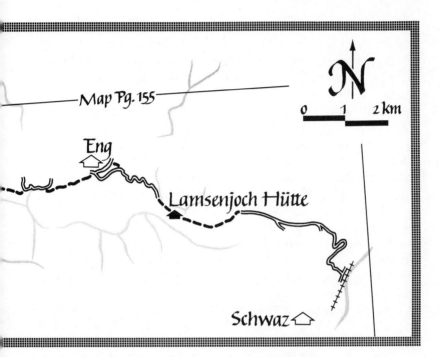

the area's riches. The area is fairly well populated with huts, although they are distributed so as to demand a few long days.

Main access is from Scharnitz or Mittenwald in the west, Schwaz or Pertisau in the east.

Map: Kompass Wanderkarte 1:50,000, sheet 26, Karwendelgebirge.

DAY 1

Scharnitz (964 m) to Brunnenstein Hütte (1560 m)

> *Time:* 2 hours
> *Distance:* 4 kilometers (2.48 miles)
> *Viewpoints:* Brunnstein Hütte
> *Access:* Scharnitz

This short hop gives you time to get to Scharnitz and ease yourself into the walking routine. If you are coming from Innsbruck, take the Mittenwald train from the *Hauptbahnhof* (main station) and get off at Scharnitz. Walk north along the main road next to the railway line, through two border posts, to enter West Germany. A couple hundred meters north of the second border post, you will find a crossing point over the railway. The crossing is marked by some red-and-white-painted metal barriers. It leads to a woodland track that heads initially for the sheer mountain face in front of you but then turns left to run parallel to the road for some way.

The sign to the Brunnenstein Hütte is at a point where the track starts to head back down towards the railway and near where the cable car serving the hut with supplies has its home base. Turn right here and head steeply up the mountain, climbing straight up at first but then following a pleasant, well-made track that zigzags fairly easily up through pine woods to the hut. It takes about one and a quarter hours to the hut from the start of the climb and is well trodden and well marked. If you are considering going on to the Tiroler Hütte, be warned, as I was, that it is *ganz klein* (very small), and has no beer.

The Brunnenstein Hütte is a little wooden cabin perched on the side of the hill. You can actually see the logs that form the walls; the lighting is run on gas from portable cylinders. It is perilously dark in the *Matratzenlager* at night and the no-flush toilets are a long way away from the hut, but it makes up for this privation in its charm and the friendly service provided by the hut warden and his wife.

DAY 2

Brunnenstein Hütte (1560 m) to Hochland Hütte (1630 m) via Linderspitzjochl (2304 m) and the Predigstuhl (1920 m)

> *Time:* 5 hours
> *Distance:* 6 kilometers (3.72 miles)
> *Viewpoints:* Predigstuhl; Linderspitzjochl
> *Access:* Karwendelbahn from Mittenwald

This is a shortish walk, possible to accomplish in not much more than half a day, but it does climb a few of the peaks along the ridge that forms the Austrian/German border. The day is spent mostly on the German side of the border, with occasional forays into Austria. The Kirchl Spitze and the Sulzliklamm Spitze provide an interesting detour on the early part of the route described here, although

Hochlandhütte 1630

Predigstuhl 1920

Dammkarhütte 1650

Westliche Karwendel
Spitze 2385

West German
Border

Linder Spitze Sudliche 2304

2

Brunnsteinhütte
1560

Sulzliklamm Spitze 2323

Kirchl Spitze 2302

Tiroler Hütte 2153

Munich

Karwendeltal

1

Scharnitz 964

Innsbruck

N

0   1   2 km

this climb may not be advisable in bad weather. Likewise, the south and north peaks of the Linderspitze and the Westliche Karwendel Spitze could provide a diversion and save you from having to spend all afternoon having lunch at the Hochland Hütte, although if the weather is nice this is a perfectly delightful thing to do. The route described here spends much of its time climbing along and around the ridge and is consequently quite steep and hazardous in places.

The climb from Brunnenstein Hütte starts off uphill through woods and then becomes very steep over rock nearer the ridge. The final thirty minutes or so is extensively cabled and in some places steel rungs are set into the rock. Some of this stretch can only be described as a scramble and should, by scrupulous local standards, be marked *nur für Geubte.* So be warned. Look out for chamois on the grassy slopes below and to your left as you climb to the pass.

From the pass, you can see long steel ladders leading down from the ridge, which is an alternative route from the Brunnenstein Hütte. Follow a painted sign on a rock at the pass that points to the cable car (the Karwendelbahn) a little to the north. After a short distance along a narrow, partially cabled path, you will reach another saddle with a sign to the *Bahn,* which is just a few minutes' walk away. There is a restaurant at the station.

The easiest, but surely not the most pleasant route from here is through a dank, cold tunnel that comes out a short way below the Westliche Karwendel Spitze and takes about five minutes to walk through. A route "over the top" is shown on the map. From the end of the tunnel, descend steeply over rock and scree past some high fences, following signs for the Dammkar Hütte. As the narrow rocky valley you have found your way into widens out, you will see a small, locked hut marked on the map as the Bergwacht Hütte. The Dammkar Hütte is visible just below, as is the road to the valley and the northern part of Mittenwald. Do not go down to the Dammkar, but take the path up over the scree to the Predigstuhl, a small promontory with a metal crucifix. This is not a peak, but is obviously a popular viewpoint because of its extensive views to the north and west. The Hochland Hütte is visible from here and takes thirty to forty minutes to reach. The initial descent is *nur für Geubte,* as the sign says, and involves slithering down some steep rock to cross a fence before trekking across a scree field. Some of this is sufficiently loose to run down — a speedy and entertaining means of descent and a way of saving the normal downhill jarring on the legs.

The Hochland Hütte had no electricity in 1985, but the interior, which has recently been modernized, includes a *Matratzenlager* of stunningly clean and beautifully worked pine. The toilets outside are spotless and the *Gaststube* is a little older but beautifully kept.

When at the hut, look out for golden eagles, which are thought to nest in the vicinity. I had an unforgettable sighting of a pair of these majestic birds gliding silently past very close to the terrace where I was sitting one sunny afternoon. They caused quite a stir among the locals, to whom they are known as *Steinadler.*

DAY 3

Hochland Hütte (1630 m) to Karwendelhaus (1771 m) via Wörner-sattel (1989 m) and Barnalpl Scharte (1819 m)

> *Time:* 5.5 hours
> *Distance:* 10 kilometers (6.2 miles)
> *Viewpoints:* Path on the side of Hochkar Spitze, Barnalpl; path on side of Karwendeltal
> *Access:* Scharnitz; Mittenwald

Today's walk involves a gradual crossing of the northern mountain ridge of the Karwendel into the Karwendeltal and so back into Austria. It joins the route most often used to cross the Karwendel from west to east and the one taken by the trans-European E4 footpath. The day begins with a sharpish climb but otherwise has gentle gradients along either side of the ridge. It is a day of great beauty, with marvelous views to the north into Germany as well as the more obvious attraction of the Karwendeltal. There is also a treat in store between the two.

The track from the Hochland Hütte leaves the eastern end of the hut (do not try going back up the track you came down yesterday) and leads along the side of the mountain through some scrubland, passing a left fork going down the hill. After twenty minutes or so, the path decides on direct confrontation with the contours and begins a fairly steep climb to the Wörnersattel. If you have a hot day in store, you should be spared the heat of the sun in the early morning because it will not yet have emerged from behind the pass.

The Wörnersattel is grassy, and seems to be used as a lavatory by large numbers of sheep. From here you can see the line of mountains you are about to walk along the side of, as well as the path that leads down the scree into the valley. Turn right, following the sign to Barnalpl and Ferein Alm. This takes you a short way along the grassy ridge before the path plunges left onto the scree. A short way down, follow the sign to the right pointing to the Karwendeltal. Do not descend further than this. Your track across the

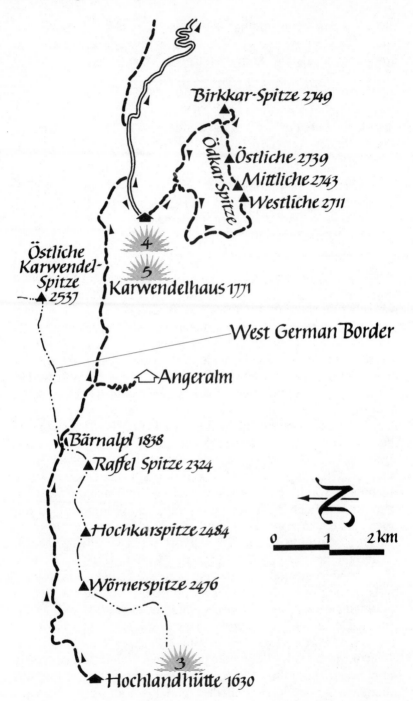

Birkkar-Spitze 2749

Ödkar Spitze

Östliche 2739
Mittliche 2743
Westliche 2711

4

5

Östliche
Karwendel-
Spitze
2537   Karwendelhaus 1771

West German Border

Angeralm

Bärnalpl 1838
Raffel Spitze 2324

N

Hochkarspitze 2484

0   1   2 km

Wörnerspitze 2476

3
Hochlandhütte 1630

scree should be clear from here and you should head for a smaller pass in a northward spur of the Hochkar Spitze. There is a steep descent from here for a short way and then a fairly straightforward mountainside traverse, with the scree runnable at various points. The usual *nur für Geubte* sign marks the beginning of the final climb to the Barnalpl Scharte; this climb requires some care, as a sheer drop quickly develops to your left.

The top of the climb marks your return to Austria, which is heralded by a small stone obelisk in the middle of the track and a metal sign saying *Staatsgrenze* (border). You are now in the Barnalpl, a grassy oasis teeming with wild flowers and butterflies that lies in a gap in the mountain ridge. This is an isolated natural wonderland where nature seems to be at her most benign and continues to flourish effortlessly, undisturbed by man. This is surely the place to stop for lunch — and don't leave your wrappers.

The track to the Karwendelhaus begins at the southern end of Barnalpl as the ground slopes steeply towards the zigzag path to Angeralm. Head downwards but do not lose too much height because you must head for a track eastwards along the mountainside. The track has great views of the valley and the mountains on the other side, but is difficult and root-strewn, running among dense, stunted pines. The Karwendelhaus is visible for most of the way, perched on a spur above some farm buildings in the middle of

Sign over the door of Karwendelhaus (Art Farash photo)

a large expanse of green pasture. Above the hut and to its left you can see a huge scree field that forms part of tomorrow's trek. There are no navigational problems in this walk and it should take about an hour and a half to reach the hut.

The Karwendelhaus is a large, pleasant place with a lovely old *Gaststube* and an excellent view of the Karwendeltal from the terrace outside. It has the feeling of being the headquarters for walkers and climbers in the region and is at the crossroads of various routes, including the E4. My experience of the hut was that the food was good, the staff pleasant, and the washing water warm. The only complaint was that food service in the *Gaststube,* whether it be for evening meal or breakfast, was extremely slow.

DAY 4

Round trip from Karwendelhaus (1771 m) to the Ödkar Spitze (2743 m) and Birkkar Spitze (2749 m)

> *Time:* 6 hours
> *Distance:* 8 kilometers (5 miles)
> *Viewpoints:* From Birkkar summit and at various points along Ödkar ridge
> *Access:* Karwendelhaus

This walk contains some very steep gradients and some tricky conditions underfoot, and so may be tough going for those who have chosen the Karwendel for its easier conditions. It takes advantage of the proximity of the Karwendelhaus to the central ridge of the Karwendel range and includes a fine ridge walk over the three peaks of the Ödkar Spitze to the highest peak in the region, the Birkkar Spitze. This excellent walk is easily done in a day; you return to the Karwendelhaus and stay a second night.

Take the well-trodden path that threads between the avalanche barriers immediately above the hut. You'll encounter a short stretch of scrambling aided by cables, but the path soon levels out to lead along the side of the valley heading south towards the Ödkar Spitze. After about fifteen minutes, take a right fork, signposted to Brendelsteig, the name of the climb you are about to make. You can see the path clearly cutting across the wide sweep of scree to your right. At the end of this you make a very steep climb out of the valley, up the side of the northwest spur of the Ödkar

Karwendelhaus as seen from the trail from Scharnitz (Art Farash photo)

Spitze. The climb is fairly well marked and trodden and parts of it are cabled. At the top, follow the ridge south for a short way and then start the steady, rocky climb around the western end of the Ödkar Spitze. You will see from this stretch the surprising barrenness of the mountainscape you are now entering.

The Ödkar Spitze consists of three peaks, named, with scrupulous Germanic logic, Westliche, Mittliche, and Östliche. The path goes over all three in that order and affords tremendous views of the Karwendeltal to the north and the mountains to the south. You also look down on the latter half of yesterday's walk, including the Barnalpl, now clearly seen as a large gap in the northern wall of the Karwendeltal.

The Mittl peak is the highest and has a cross with a small metal box containing a visitors' book. This point should be reached in about three and a half hours from the hut. The Birkkar Spitze is immediately to the east and behind it is the Kaltwasserkar Spitze. After going over the Östliche peak, you must descend from the high point of the ridge to the Schlauchkarsattel. This is a dangerous stretch, with steep drops on either side — particularly to the north — and with very loose rock underfoot. Much of it is cabled and demands lowering yourself down very carefully.

At the much-frequented saddle you will see the path going down the valley to your left. Continue straight on, passing the ridiculous Birkkar Hütte (literally balanced on a ridge and held down by cables set into the mountain), and begin the short climb

Halleranger Hütte lies along an alternate route connecting Karwendelhaus and Innsbruck. (Franz Nussbaumer photo)

to the Birkkar Spitze, which has a large cross on top. The most striking view from the peak is of the Ödkar ridge; it's very satisfying to get this overview of the rocky ridge you have just painstakingly negotiated.

Go back down to the saddle and begin your descent into the valley, which leads to the hut and which you were able to see as a towering backdrop to the hut from the other side of the Karwendel-tal yesterday. The initial descent of this is probably the most difficult part of the whole walk, being very loose and steep, with a mixture of scree and mud underfoot; its condition is exacerbated by the large number of people who walk here. It is quite well marked, although you should watch carefully for the red marks. Eventually the scree becomes runnable and this is a great relief after the cautious sliding and jarring of the first stretch. It is a relief also to the eye to get back onto mountainside with some vegetation after such a long time among unrelieved rock. You'll soon pass the sign to the Brendelsteig at which you turned right on your way up. This means you're nearly home and it is only fifteen minutes or so from here to the hut.

Alternate route: If you wish, break the west-east crossing at the Karwendelhaus and turn south, making the tough climb to the Slauchkarsattel and climbing the Birkkar Spitze before continuing south to the Halleranger Hütte. From here, the route runs south-west via the Stempljoch, Pfeis Hütte, and Mannl Scharte before getting to Hafelekar Bergot, where a funicular railway runs down to the outskirts of Innsbruck.

DAY 5

Karwendelhaus (1771 m) to Lamsenjoch Hütte (1953 m) via Falken Hütte (1846 m) and Eng (1216 m)

Time: 8 hours
Distance: 16 kilometers (9.92 miles)
Viewpoints: Falken Hütte; Eng
Access: Eng

If you wish, this long day's walk can be broken at Eng, making tomorrow's concluding stretch correspondingly longer. However, accommodation will certainly be more expensive at Eng than at the

The Falken Hütte (Adolf Sotier Haus) (Art Farash photo)

Lamsenjoch Hütte, and the hut itself is a very pleasant place to stay. Except for the final climb to the hut, this is a day of gentle gradients through pleasant wooded valleys and across grassland — quite the opposite of yesterday's rocky trek.

Follow the main track eastwards from the Karwendelhaus. You can stay on it almost all the way to the Falken Hütte or branch off left not long after the Hochalmsattel and rejoin it in the valley at Pürschaus. Follow the sign to the Falken Hütte there, turning right to cross a stream bed, and climb steadily up the hill, past a farmhouse at Ladiz Alpe. A short way after this you will find a track on the left signed to the Falken Hütte that leads over some grassland. You can just see the roof of the hut from the bottom of this final, gradual climb. This small hut is set against a stunning backdrop of mountains, including the Laliderer Spitze. You should reach it in two and a half to three hours.

From the hut you can see both the track leading east along the side of the Laliderer Spitze to the Hohljoch and the road below it zigzagging to get to the same place. Follow the main track from the hut, which leads west initially, and then pick up the footpath going east. You get good views of the Dreizinken Spitze from the Hohljoch. Follow the sign down a well-trodden footpath to Eng. As you round the mountainside, the orange blinds of a large hotel

Schwaz

Innsbruck

Stallental

6 Lamsenjochhütte 1953

Alpengasthof
Eng 1218 Binsalm 1502

Eng

Hohljoch 1795

Falkenhütte
1846 Laliderer Spitze 2582

Pürschaus 1403

0   2   4 km

The Falken Hütte is 2-1/2 hours from Karwendelhaus. (Art Farash photo)

make Eng very conspicuous from far up the valley. Eng is, as the blinds suggest, a tourist resort, but one that has been well protected from the usual ravages of the tourist trade.

Before tourism, Eng's lifeblood was dairy cattle; they are still important, as evidenced by the neat line of milking parlors and stables at one end of the village. The cattle graze in a wide flat valley divided by wooden fences, and set off by magnificent mountains. The scene is fairly typical, but there is something especially impressive about Eng — and this has not escaped the notice of the developers. However, they have somehow been restrained from filling the valley with tourist traps, the only traces of which are discreetly positioned at one end of the valley.

Food and drink are available from the cafe or the *Gasthof* at the north end of the village; the *Wurst,* bread, and buttermilk are worth trying. It is a wonderful surprise to find decent bread in Austria.

The path to the Lamsenjoch Hütte starts near the "business" end of Eng. It goes up next to the stream for a short way and then turns steeply through woods to join the main track to Binsalm and the Lamsenjoch. This steady trudge follows the zigzags of the car-size track, past the cafe at Binsalm and up the middle of the valley. You can cut some corners by taking the tracks across the grass and scrub. The climb is generally not steep, but it is a relief to go through the gate marking the westliche Lamsenjoch, where you can see the hut a short distance away, along a level stretch of mountainside.

The Lamsenjoch Hütte is an excellent place to spend your last night in the Karwendel. The staff is very welcoming and there is a very pleasant *Gaststube* to eat and relax in after your long walk.

DAY 6

Lamsenjoch Hütte (1953 m) to Schwaz (538 m)

> *Time:* 3.5 hours
> *Distance:* 10 kilometers (6.2 miles)
> *Viewpoints:* The track down from Lamsenjoch Hütte
> *Access:* Schwaz

This easy walk will get you to the Inn Valley and the railway station by lunchtime if you leave around 9 A.M. If you have time to spare, you may want to climb the Lamsenspitze, which can be reached by a marked path from the Lamsenjoch Hütte. The way down to Schwaz is on a stony but well-trodden track that winds gently down the valley, below cliffs and through wooded areas. The path follows the Stallenbach for a while, then joins a farm track, and eventually leads to a paved road above Schwaz.

You can see the river and a motorway as you make the final descent. You come out by a church, and turn left down the hill, going under the motorway. The railway station is a few hundred meters away.

After a tour of such beauty, a sense of anticlimax may descend with you into the valley. You hear the increasing roar of *Autobahn* traffic and catch occasional glimpses of buildings, road, and flat fields through the trees on the way down. Even after spending the best part of a week in the mountains, the prospect of a bath and a proper bed may seem less appealing when you realize their price is the peace and beauty of the high Alps.

~TOUR 8~

The Venediger Hohenweg

Route: *Ströden – Essener-Rostocker Hütte –
Johannis Hütte – Eissee Hütte – Bonn-Matreier Hütte –
Badener Hütte – Venediger Haus – Matreier Tauernhaus*

In the western part of the Höhe Tauern, the Venediger Group, dominated by Grossvenediger (3674 meters) is an area of heavy glaciation with the largest covering of ice in the eastern Alps. This makes for very dramatic scenery: snow-covered ice with gray-blue bulges scarred and cut by menacing crevasses. The landscape was carved out by massive glaciers during the ice ages, leaving broad valleys too wide for the streams in them and rocks that have been shattered, sculpted, and scratched by the ice and washed by the weather over thousands of years. The glaciers have also left boulder fields, tons of rock dumped by the melting ice.

The existing glaciers can be glimpsed at the head of each of the many valleys, which radiate from the central frozen mass of the Venediger Group. Each glacier issues a melt stream into the boulders and a mess of glacial debris. On this walk, shattered rocks of many different colors can be seen to the south in the Lasörling Group and on all the passes that the Venediger Hohenweg crosses.

South from Defreggerhaus (George Neffinger photo)

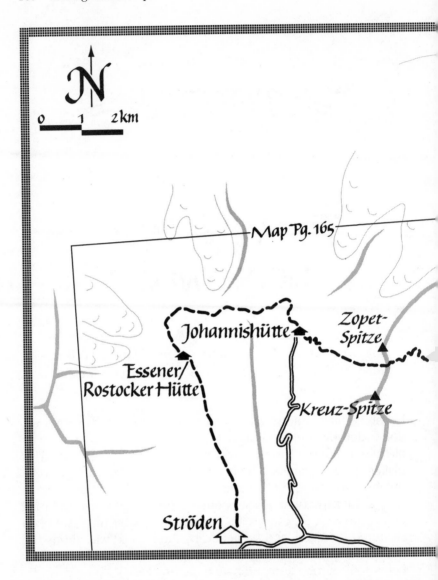

The Venediger Hohenweg is a high-level path connecting Alpine Club huts. Strangely, the official path starts in the Lasörling Group at the Neue Reichenberger Hütte to the south of the Virgental, quite a distance from the Venediger. It then descends into the Umbaltal (at the head of Virgental) before starting its journey

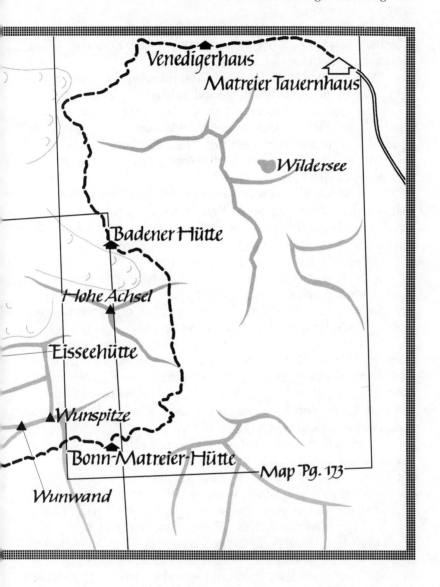

around the south and east of the group, visiting huts high up in the side valleys and joining the valleys by climbs of high, wild passes.

From Clara Hütte in Umbaltal, the route to Essener-Rostocker Hütte is now considered dangerous. This, and the desire to concentrate the walk on the Venediger, means that the walk misses the excursion into the Lasörling Group and that dangerous glacier crossing and starts by going directly to the Essener-Rostocker Hütte to join the Venediger Hohenweg.

From Essener-Rostocker Hütte, the route goes east along the south side of the mountain range and then north along its eastern edge. The south side is drained by a number of parallel valleys, the Maurer Tal, the Dorfer Tal, Timmeltal, and Niltal, each of which has a hut high up in its furthest reaches. The walks between them are over the intervening ridges and across shattered and, in bad weather, inhospitable passes.

Each day's walk is not long and time can be taken to enjoy the magnificence of the mountains. Early in the season the mountainsides are a mass of blue and yellow Alpine flowers; you can also see the famous edelweiss along this route.

Paths are well marked and well maintained and the walking is easy underfoot except over the passes, which may have snow patches even in late summer. However, the paths are obvious and, provided one has reasonable visibility and good equipment, these passes should be quickly and safely crossed.

As all the huts are in side valleys, it is possible on each day to drop down from the high-level route to escape bad weather or to visit towns. The only place that the route may force an unintended descent to the valley for an easier way around is at Galten Scharte, just past Bonn-Matreier Hütte, if the pass is in particularly bad condition, as described on Day 5.

All the valleys on the south side descend to, or at least near, a village where food and accommodation will be available. However, if a descent of Frosnitztal on the east side is forced on you, it leads only to a bus stop at Gruben. Matrei is only a short bus ride from there, but the service is not frequent in the Tauerntal and it would be a long day out from Badener Hütte to go shopping in Matrei.

Matrei is the focal point for the start and finish of the walk. It is possible to get buses there from Mittersill in Salzachtal in the north or from Lienz in the south and from Matrei to Ströden to start the walk. Similarly, the bus from Matreier Tauernhaus at the end goes to Matrei, with the same choice of homeward journeys.

The Grossvenediger is at the center of the week's outing. It is the hub of the wheel of valleys and ridges and dominates both the views and the thoughts of climbers and walkers. It is not a difficult peak to ascend in Alpine climbing terms, but walkers should hire a guide to negotiate its many crevasses. You may arrange for a guide's

Along the trail between Johannis Hütte and Defreggerhaus, on the way to Grossvenediger (George Neffinger photo)

services at any of the tourist information offices in the villages or even through a hut warden if he has radio contact with the central office in Matrei. The best way to arrange a guided ascent of the Grossvenediger during this walk is by the "normal" southern route from Defregger Haus. Instead of stopping overnight at the Johannis Hütte, walkers wishing to climb the Grossvenediger would walk on two hours to the Defregger Haus, where they would meet the guide the next morning. He would then take you to the summit via Rainer Törl and the Oberer Kees Boden. You could then descend to the Johannis Hütte for the night and continue with the itinerary from there. This is a most exciting and rewarding day on the glaciers, particularly if the views are clear.

Overall, the route is at a high level; once you reach the Essener-Rostocker Hütte the path does not go below 2000 meters until the final descent. Such a huge mountain mass as the Grossvenediger makes its own weather, and the wind off the glaciers can be extremely cold. The cooling effect of the glaciers can also make mist and cloud hang around the group for longer than is normally expected. Therefore, you should take plenty of warm clothing for this walk as well as the usual waterproofs. A good map and compass are also required, especially in case of mist.

Map: Alpine Club 1:25,000, sheet 36 (Venediger Gruppe). Make sure you get an up-to-date edition showing the Sajat and Eissee huts and their connecting paths. If this map is not available, a good alternative is sheet 123 (Defreggen and Virgental).

DAY 1

Ströden (1403 m) to Essener-Rostocker Hütte (2208 m)

Time: 3 hours
Distance: 7 kilometers (4.34 miles)
Viewpoints: Essener-Rostocker Hütte
Access: Ströden

The Virgental runs west from Matrei in Osttirol and separates the shaly Lasörling Group in the south from the starkly contrasting Venediger Group to the north. The weird rock forms of the Lasörling Group are mirrored by some of the south-lying mountains of the Venediger Group, but it is the large expanses of glaciers, ice, and snow that impress the traveler in the Venediger. At the end of the road into the Virgental lies Ströden, which is the terminus for valley buses that run from Lienz via Huben and Matrei in Iseltal.

The route to Essener-Rostocker Hütte from Ströden is north up the Maurer Tal and is well marked and easy to follow. It starts on a broad track on the west side of the stream (the Maurer Bach) and leads to Stoanalm, where you can get refreshments. Near here is a bridge where the track recrosses the stream at approximately 1460 meters. An alternative path cuts through the woods from the back

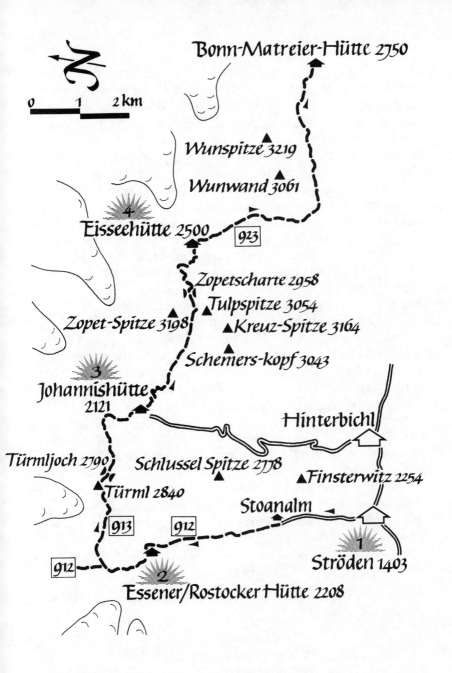

of the parking area that joins the track at Stoanalm, but it is steep and muddy in places. Stoanalm is the last opportunity before the hut to buy drinks.

From Stoanalm the track continues 1 kilometer up the valley to the bottom of the cable car used to supply the hut. It is possible to have rucksacks transported to the hut this way. The track ends here; you now follow a narrow path on the east side of the stream, climbing the hillside a little to get above a ravine where the water tumbles down in impressive falls. At about 2000 meters the valley flattens out again and a short distance higher the path crosses onto the same side as the Essener-Rostocker Hütte. Continue alongside the stream on somewhat more rocky terrain until the path swings left and zigzags up through boulders and rock outcrops to the hut.

Essener-Rostocker Hütte is situated on a side moraine where, in ages past, the Simonykees glacier flowed into the Maurerkees glacier. Both glaciers have long since retreated into their respective valleys, leaving a wonderful position for the hut — on a lip at the entrance to an amphitheater of mountains and glaciers.

Take a short stroll from the hut up the south lateral moraine left by Simonykees (towards Rostock Eck) to really appreciate the magnitude and magnificence of these mountains: the shimmering peaks of Simony Spitze and Grosser Geiger, the dark menacing ice showing through the snow, the rocky wastelands broken up and laid bare by the receding glaciers — this is the world of the Venediger Group.

The hut (or huts) is a bit of an anomaly. The old Rostocker Hütte was built in 1912 in the traditional style, and the Essener Hütte was added to it as a larger and more modern building in 1966. The original Essener Hütte in Umbaltal was destroyed by an avalanche in 1935 and the rebuilt Neue Essener Hütte was swept away in 1958. The two adjoining huts stand side by side in sharp contrast.

DAY 2

Essener-Rostocker Hütte (2208 m) to Johannis Hütte (2121 m) via Türmljoch (2790 m)

Time: 3.5 hours
Distance: 6 kilometers (3.72 miles)
Viewpoints: Turmljoch
Access: Ströden/Hinterbichl

The route from Essener-Rostocker Hütte to Johannis Hütte is not difficult and is well marked throughout. However, it does go up

Resting at Turmljoch (George Neffinger photo)

quite high over Türmljoch and may have some late snow patches.

From the hut, go a little way north along the west side of the stream into the rocky wastes of upper Maurer Tal, over and around boulders and streams. The path to Türmljoch is called the Schweriner Weg and heads generally east from where it crosses the main stream in Maurer Tal. It passes two junctions, both side paths to the left; the first is a climbers' path to the Simony Spitzen and the second, met just after crossing the stream, goes into the back of the valley and eventually to the Grosser Geiger or over Maurertorl to Warnsdorfer Hütte.

On the Schweriner Weg the going is fairly rough underfoot on the boulders in the valley bottom, but it becomes firmer and the path is more obvious as it climbs. It goes steeply up through boulders and around the back of a small side stream valley, then onto the sparse vegetation of the more open hillside. As it passes south of the long, broken, rocky south ridge of Grosser Happ, the path turns more northerly and zigzags up a grassy slope. But as the way turns east again and heads up to the pass, it is once more over rocky terrain and is marked with stone cairns as well as the familiar paint splashes.

Türmljoch is the point on our route that separates Maurer Tal from Dorfer Tal, where the Johannis Hütte is located. To reach the hut, descend from the pass, still in an easterly direction, over broken rocks and perhaps some lingering snow patches, through terraces on the side of the valley and on to the bare cliffs of Aderkamm. This is passed on the north end and the path immediately turns south through boulder-strewn slopes. Go down to a bridge across the Dorfer Bach, where a polished gorge has been carved out by the water, and across the meadows to Johannis Hütte, on the south bank of the Zettalunitz Bach. Just before you reach the hut, you will join the well-worn path that connects Johannis Hütte with the popular Defregger Haus.

Johannis Hütte is the oldest (over a century) as well as one of the smallest huts on the Venediger Hohenweg. Nowadays there is a road up Dorfer Tal to the hut and it has many day visitors. The temptation has so far been resisted to "cash in" on those day visitors and to extend the hut until it becomes just another restaurant/cafe. Long may it retain its Old World charm and character. The parking area at the end of the road may be full and the hut thronged with people when you arrive, but do not worry. The parking area also serves the Defregger Haus and its constant crowd. The day visitors will be making their way back to Virgental come the late afternoon, leaving you to enjoy this quaint and charming hostelry in peace and quiet.

DAY 3

Johannis Hütte (2121 m) to Eissee Hütte (2500 m) via Zopetscharte (2958 m)

Time: 4 hours
Distance: 5 kilometers (3.1 miles)
Viewpoints: Zopetscharte
Access: Prägraten/Hinterbichl

From Johannis Hütte the Venediger Hohenweg goes fairly steeply up to Zopetscharte and from there descends, sometimes a little awkwardly and with a steel wire or two put in for security, to Eissee Hütte. Zopetscharte is a high, wild place that can be very bleak and inhospitable in bad weather. But the path is well marked and should be obvious in all but the thickest mist or heaviest rain.

Snow patches may still cover portions of path in late summer.
(Art Farash photo)

If the weather is bad, you may be tempted to try an alternative route to the Eissee Hütte via the new Sajat Hütte. However, it is just as treacherous underfoot and does not really offer an alternative bad-weather route.

Head east from the Johannis Hütte on the south side of Zettalunitz Bach. Go steeply up and away from the stream bank to cut around the mountainside. The path is unrelentingly steep but the higher one gets, the more magnificent the view to the north becomes as more and more of Grossvenediger becomes visible. At least the view is a good excuse to keep stopping on this steep, grassy mountainside.

The path branches high on the side of the valley. The right-hand path leads over Feldscharte to Sajat Hütte; take the left-hand one, which zigzags up a slope and into a narrow side valley. It stays reasonably level on a well-trodden shale path, and then steeply zigzags up on loose stones to the cairn on the narrow Zopetscharte.

The views that greet you as you approach the pass are stupendous, revealing not only the strange rock formations in the vicinity of the pass itself, but also the mighty mountains around the Timmeltal, particularly Weiss Spitze and Eichham, protruding from the glistening glaciers, and the shattered rocky ridges that climb to the peaks out of deserts of boulders.

The path down from Zopetscharte is somewhat steep and rough and you have to use a hand in one or two places; there are some steel wires to hang onto as the path winds its way down. Soon the way again lies through boulder-strewn slopes, eventually taking you along the west bank of the Timmelbach to a bridge that carries the path from Eissee Hütte to Wallhorntorl. Cross over the stream on the bridge and follow this path back down the valley, past a junction with a path to Eissee Lake, and slightly uphill round a left corner to the hut.

Eissee Hütte has only recently been built. It is very comfortable and, after Johannis Hütte, seems very modern in decor and style. It is privately owned but is run along the same lines as an Alpine Club hut, except that it has only dormitory accommodations — no bedrooms.

DAY 4

Eissee Hütte (2500 m) to Bonn-Matreier Hütte (2750 m)

Time: 4.5 hours
Distance: 6.5 kilometers (4.03 miles)
Viewpoints: Generally southwards
Access: Virgen/Prägraten

This route is well marked all the way and easy to follow, but it does have a couple of nasty, steep surprises.

Take the path from the door of Eissee Hütte around the back of the valley; it stays at much the same altitude as the hut. The path maintains a southeasterly direction as it weaves in and out across the grassy flanks. Keep a lookout for the red paint dabs, as there are misleading sheep tracks around here that can tempt the unwary to stray from the narrow Venediger Hohenweg.

The route takes many turns, usually bearing left, as it goes around the slopes of Wun Spitze. Just after the first turn, as the path starts to rise again, you pass a side path that goes steeply down to the right to Wallhorn Alm and can also be joined from Sajat Hütte. Keep high on the side of Wun Spitze, going in and out over minor ridges as the path turns east. Wun Alm, a farm, comes into view below the path on the slopes of the valley side and is passed by as the path goes down a bit on rocks and around the back of a slight bowl to come to the first of the surprises. Yes, you really must go up

Bonn-Matreier Hütte along the Venediger Hohenweg (George Neffinger photo)

the short but so steep slope, up to an obvious depression in the rocky south ridge of Wun Spitze.

The path levels again around the back of another valley and in one large zigzag climbs onto a saddle on the Esels Rücken ("donkey's back"), as this ridge is called. Here is the second surprise: a steep narrow gully down the east side of the ridge, which has a loose stony surface. However, a firm path has been built in zigzags down it to the boulder field in the back of the Niltal. Having descended the nasty but short gully, the path turns left over the boulders around the back of the valley to join the path that comes up Niltal from Virgen to Bonn-Matreier Hütte. From this junction the way is up on rocks in a series of curves, the last of which brings the walker above cliffs and out onto an easy, grassy path for the last few meters to the hut.

Bonn-Matreier Hütte is pleasantly situated and comfortable — even hot showers are available. It is under the control of two different Alpine Clubs. Behind the hut is a shrine dedicated to some youths who lost their lives in a mountaineering accident not far away — a grim reminder of how demanding even these mountains can be and of how careful one needs to be to walk among them safely.

DAY 5

Bonn-Matreier Hütte (2750 m) to Badener Hütte (2608 m) via Kalber Scharte (2791 m) and Galten Scharte (2882 m)

Time: 6 hours
Distance: 8.5 kilometers (5.27 miles)
Viewpoints: Galten Scharte
Access: Gruben/Virgen

This day contains potentially the most dangerous part of the whole walk — the crossing of Galten Scharte. Although it is not particularly difficult and when dry presents no problems, the surface on the descent from Galten Scharte to Mailfrosnitzbach is, in places, very loose. It is composed of fine shale, which can become very slippery if the mountainside is running with water after recent rain or if snow is lying on it. In addition, the descent is very steep and there is the ever-present danger of loosened stones falling or being dislodged by careless parties above yours. Obtain the advice of the warden at Bonn-Matreier Hütte if you have doubts about the conditions likely to be encountered.

If there has been recent bad weather or if a lot of snow is still lingering on the route, it may be better to allow discretion to win the day and to retreat down Niltal to Virgen for a bus to Matrei. There you can take another bus up Tauerntal to Gruben (1164 meters), and from there you can undertake a long walk up Frossnitztal to join today's route at Achsel (2225 meters). There is bus service between Virgen and Gruben.

Let us assume, however, that the sun is shining and that the paths are quite dry. Take the path behind the Bonn-Matreier Hütte up onto a ridge of higher ground and around the valley to a pass, Kalber Scharte, on another ridge coming down from Rauh Kopf to the east of the hut. Just before the path goes down to the back of this valley, a climbers' path to the left is passed; it goes to Sail Kopf and Hoher Eichham. Similarly, just before turning a corner on some rocks directly below Kalber Scharte, you pass another marked path on the left, this time to Rauh Kopf. The pass is very narrow and the path descends immediately onto a boulder field and contours around on this to once again zigzag up on rocks to Galten Scharte.

The path from Galten Scharte is well marked and *must* be adhered to — it is the only feasible way to descend a very difficult

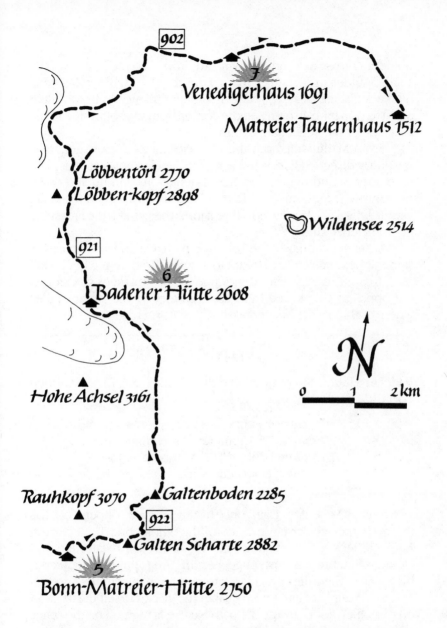

902

7
Venedigerhaus 1691

Matreier Tauernhaus 1512

Löbbentörl 2770
▲ **Löbben-kopf 2898**

⬭ **Wildensee 2514**

921

6
Badener Hütte 2608

N

0   1   2 km

▲ **Hohe Achsel 3161**

▲ **Galtenboden 2285**

Rauhkopf 3070
▲

922

▲ **Galten Scharte 2882**

5
Bonn-Matreier-Hütte 2750

mountainside. The path is constantly zigzagging and has many sudden changes of direction to get around some difficult terrain or to take advantage of a slightly less steep slope. It goes east from the pass on a path of fine shale under some rather imposing cliffs and is equipped with some steel wires. It then zigzags down a bit of a "nose" in a more northerly direction and on reaching the inevitable boulders turns west and finally north down into the bottom of the small boulder-strewn valley that carries the stream below Mailfrosnitzkees glacier. In all you descend about 600 meters from Galten Scharte. You have also turned the corner from the south side to the east side of the Venediger Group.

From Mailfrosnitzbach the path continues its now generally northerly direction fairly level across the rocky mountainside. The path goes in and out around side indentations and up and down over minor ridges, but stays level or slightly downhill to the small lake at Achsel (2225 meters). Here it joins the path up the Frossnitztal to Badener Hütte.

At the junction take the left-hand path, which leads up across stony slopes and across a stream to a steep climb up the high bank of a stream (also the lateral moraine of Frossnitzkees glacier) on the opposite side to the hut. Lastly, go around the stream valley when just below the hut and easily up to its very welcome shelter.

DAY 6

Badener Hütte (2608 m) to Venediger Haus (1691 m) via Löbben Törl (2770 m)

Time: 4 hours
Distance: 7.5 kilometers (4.65 miles)
Viewpoints: Löbben Törl to Innergschlöss
Access: Tauerntal

The route to Venediger Haus, once having crossed Löbben Törl, has the most spectacular close views of the whole tour. The Schlaten Kees glacier's ice is hanging onto the sides of Kristallwand and Hoher Zaun, but only just; huge ice cliffs are toppling imperceptibly towards the valley, cracking into deep translucent blue crevasses as the weight of its own ice pushes the glacier to self-destruction on the valley floor. Luckily the path we use is high up on the other side of the valley, rocky but safe.

From Badener Hütte, the path goes generally north and contours along the rocky slopes. However, some rocky ridges are a little more tricky and care has to be exercised to ensure a safe passage down from their crests.

Grossvenediger from Messlina Scharte (George Neffinger photo)

A right-hand side path to Wilden Kogel is passed and immediately the path starts its climb up to Löbben Törl, the pass between Löbben Kogel and Innerer Knorrkogel. On the pass a striking crucifix has been erected. With the magnificent view across Schlaten Kees and with the summit of Grossvenediger as a backdrop, it makes an inspiring picture.

The route down from the pass is subject to late-lying snow patches, but the path should be easy to see and to follow as it contours northward across boulders and scree and then zigzags down rather steeply and rockily to the lateral moraine on the east side of the glacier. The top of this hogsback of glacial debris is

Edelweiss (Bob & Ira Spring photo)

followed as it turns right towards the lakes to Salzboden and passes two paths across to the Prager Hütte on the far bank. At Salzboden the path zigzags down through rocks to the tracks on the floor of the seemingly wide and green Gschlösstal. Follow the track on either side of the stream down to Innergschlöss, the hamlet in which the Venediger Haus is to be found.

The whole section from Löbben Törl to Innergschlöss is dominated by views of Schlaten Kees glacier, from the awesome icefalls high up near the pass to the picturesque long-distance views of the snows seen from the lower valley. The summit of Grossvenediger from this angle is just discernible as a slight hump of snow in the vast snowfields that surround it.

DAY 7

Venediger Haus (1691 m) to Matreier Tauernhaus (1512 m)

Time: 1.5 hours
Distance: 5.5 kilometers (3.41 miles)
Viewpoints: Scenery on the Venediger Hohenweg
Access: Tauerntal

The descent from the high paths of the Venediger Hohenweg was really done on the previous day coming down to Innergschlöss. This short day merely leads to the bus stop at Matreier Tauernhaus and so back to civilization.

The walk from Venediger Haus to Matreier Tauernhaus is easily done on the wide track, almost a road, on the north side of the stream, and gives plenty of time to ponder on the proposed

Huts are scattered throughout the Venediger Alps. (George Neffinger photo)

damming and flooding of this beautiful valley and time to recollect the magnificent scenery enjoyed on this walk on the Venediger Hohenweg.

It is a one-and-a-half-hour bus ride from Matreier Tauernhaus back to Lienz or just over an hour, changing at Matrei, to get to the parking area at Ströden. Buses depart several times a day, through late afternoon. A party wishing to get back quickly could carry on from Venediger Haus without stopping overnight and be in time for the last bus, if they left Badener Hütte early enough. But a rush on the last day can spoil the entire walk and a leisurely stroll down the valley to Matreier Tauernhaus on the seventh day is much more pleasant. Besides, catching an earlier bus probably means a more convenient arrival time in Lienz or wherever you are going.

TOUR 9

The Grossglockner and Schober Groups

Route: *(Zell-am-See) — Dr. Adolf Scharf Haus —*
Rudolfs Hütte — Kalser Tauernhaus — Studl Hütte —
Glorer Hütte — Elberfelder Hütte — Lienzer Hütte —
Wangenitzsee Hütte — Mörtschach

The central portion of the Höhe Tauern (south of Zell-am-See) is famous for containing Grossglockner (3798 meters), the highest peak in Austria. Sharply pointed and "peaky" from any angle, the mountain is imposing and magnificent. Surprisingly, Grossglockner is not strictly on the main Alpine ridge running across Europe, but is at the end of a side ridge jutting out to the south. This ridge has large glaciers on both sides of it, including Pasterze glacier, the longest single glacier in the eastern Alps. The whole of the Grossglockner massif is well covered with ages-old ice.

Immediately to the south of the Grossglockner group and joined to it at Peischlach Törl is the Schober group. While still part of the Höhe Tauern, it contrasts with its northern neighbor's style of scenery: the Schober group consists of stark mountains of shattered rock, dry and dark in comparison to the glistening glaciers of Glockner.

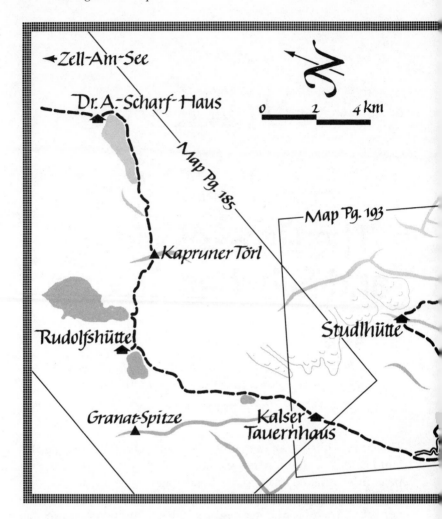

This walk through the two groups starts from near Kaprun in the north of the Grossglockner group and skirts around the main mass of the glaciers on the north and west sides before going to the heart of the group, to Studl Hütte, right at the foot of Grossglockner itself. Our tour then turns south into the Schober group, twisting around its ridges to Mörtschach in Mölltal. The scenery throughout is superb: the drama of high Alpine peaks, near and far; the hanging glaciers to be seen in the Grossglockner group; the gentle Alpine meadows around Lienzer Hütte in the Schober group and that group's rocky yet friendly mountains. Every day is different.

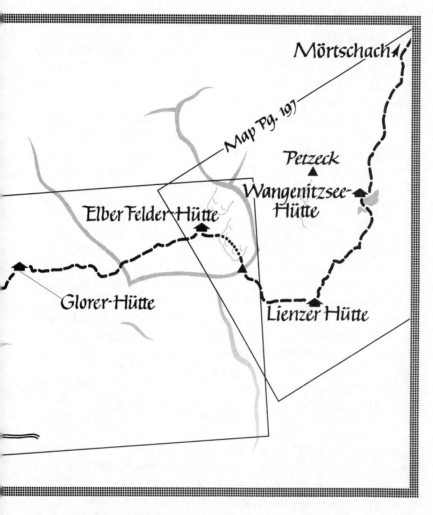

A great diversity of style is also shown by the huts — from the drab concrete modernity of Dr. Adolf Scharf Haus to the thriving hotel trade at Rudolfs Hütte; from the impersonal bustle of a "single-purpose" establishment at Studl Hütte (for would-be conquerors of Grossglockner) to the genuine cozy welcome at Kalser Tauernhaus, Elberfelder Hütte, and Glorer Hütte, to the comforts of the Lienzer and Wangenitzsee huts.

The walking has its contrasts too: short days between closely situated huts and some long hauls out of one valley into another. But no day is too long to put this tour out of the scope or abilities of the average fit walker. However, the majority of the walking is at a high level, frequently going over high passes, and one must expect awkward and rough conditions underfoot. The few dangerous spots are made safer by steel wires or ladders. Anyone undertaking this walk should be used to walking in mountains and should know how to navigate from map and compass.

The basic walk lasts nine days but this could be reduced by combining one or two of the shorter days with others to make what would be to most walkers prohibitively long stretches. The walk from Studl Hütte to Glorer Hütte, for instance, could conceivably be continued on to Elberfelder Hütte. It would also be feasible to go from Lienzer Hütte to Mörtschach in a day without stopping overnight at Wangenitzsee Hütte; however, in this case the walker would probably reach Mörtschach too late to take advantage of public transport.

There are access points to or from this route at each hut, so it would also be possible to shorten the route to a week by joining it or leaving it partway along. These access points also make convenient places to shop or visit if you are being plagued by bad weather higher up. It is possible, especially by using the cable car, to get to Enzingerboden from Rudolfs Hütte and from there by bus to Uttendorf in Salzachtal. Buses also run to Uttendorf from the Zell-am-See railway station. On these buses, run by the Oster-reichische Bundesbahn (Austrian State Railways), fares are reduced for members of the Alpine Club. It is a simple matter to walk down to Kals from Kalser Tauernhaus, Studl Hütte, or Glorer Hütte and you can get to Heiligenblut from Glorer Hütte and Elberfelder Hütte. Buses run to Lienz from both Kals and Heiligenblut and even to Zell-am-See from Heiligenblut. An easy four-and-a-half-hour walk brings you down to Lienz from Lienzer Hütte. Any of these escape routes can be used in reverse to join the route further along or as a way to spend a day or two away from the rigors of the "high life."

The weather in these mountains is very changeable — a group the nature and size of Grossglockner makes its own weather — so do be prepared for the worst, although the short summer season around the Höhe Tauern can have long spells of clear fine weather. The best time of year for doing this tour is late July to early September.

Maps: The 1:25,000 series produced by the Alpine Club, sheets 40

Resting along a cold mountain stream (Tyrolean National Tourist Office, Innsbruck, photo)

(Grossglocknergruppe) and 41 (Schobergruppe). Freytag and Berndt make a good 1:50,000 series; sheets 122 (Grossglockner, Kaprun, Zell-am-See) and 181 (Lienz, Heiligenblut, Matrei) would cover the walk.

DAY 1

By bus from Zell-am-See to Dr. Adolf Scharf Haus (2112 m)

Since the construction of the hydroelectric works in Kapruner Tal, with its reservoirs and roads, there is no reasonable way for the foot traveler to gain access up the valley. So, unfortunately, the first day is spent on buses and a lift getting to Dr. Adolf Scharf Haus, but it does allow plenty of time to enjoy the stunning scenery around Stausee Mooserboden, the reservoir on whose dam Dr. Adolf Scharf Haus stands.

Zell-am-See has a main-line railway station with trains from Innsbruck, Munich, Salzburg, and the south. Buses run from the bus station, located just on the uphill side of the town center, via a stop at the railway station to Kaprun and further into Kapruner Tal up to Stausee Mooserboden. From Kaprun the road winds steeply up into the narrow, steep-sided valley below the dam of the first reservoir. Here an open-air platform on rails takes its standing passengers up the mountainside to another road at the height of the reservoir. A bus ride alongside this reservoir through tunnels and around hairpin bends brings you to Moosersperre, the dam of the second reservoir, and to Dr. Adolf Scharf Haus.

The hut is, in fact, the lighthouse-like structure at the far end of this dam, on a rock projection between the two dams that contain the waters of Stausee Mooserboden. It is a popular place and it would be advisable to book your beds for the night as early as possible, either on arrival or by phone from Kaprun or Zell-am-See (the phone number is 82 710). It is owned by the Touristenverein Naturfreunde, so Alpine Club members cannot expect preferential treatment in the allocation of beds.

The scenery around the Mooserboden reservoir consists of the high glaciated mountains that enclose this man-made lake high in the back of the valley. It is truly breathtaking and one can only wonder how much more spectacular it must have seemed before the damming (damning?) of the valley.

DAY 2

Dr. Adolf Scharf Haus (2112 m) to Rudolfs Hütte (2315 m) via Kapruner Törl (2639 m)

Time: 6 hours
Distance: 12 kilometers (7.44 miles)
Viewpoints: Kapruner Törl
Access: Kapruner Tal

Your first day of walking is a fairly tough one, passing over rough terrain in high mountains.

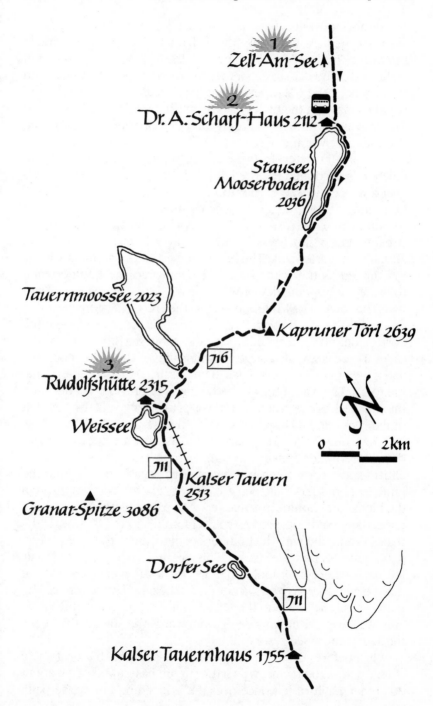

1 Zell-Am-See ▲

2 Dr. A. Scharf-Haus 2112 ▲

Stausee Mooserboden 2036

Tauernmoossee 2023

Kapruner Törl 2639

716

3 Rudolfshütte 2315 ▲

Weissee

711

Kalser Tauern 2513

▲ Granat-Spitze 3086

N

0   1   2 km

Dorfer See

711

Kalser Tauernhaus 1755 ▲

From Dr. Adolf Scharf Haus turn left along the dams to the east side of the reservoir and take the path on the east and south side of the water. This involves climbing over the wall of the pump station at the end of the dam to get onto the path, which starts along an old track. Where the track peters out in a stream bed the red paint splashes marking the path are easily picked up. The path is easy to follow along the side of the reservoir but it does tend to go up and down to get over any obstacles.

About 400 meters from the western end of the reservoir, a path junction is encountered. The left-hand path is little used and leads over a very crevassed glacier to Riffltor and to Oberwalder Hütte. Our path continues to a bridge across the stream that feeds down the valley into the reservoir. Go steeply up the north side of the stream; after a short way turn right, away from the stream, and zigzag up a grassy bank. The height gained on the mountainside is maintained as the path heads southwest into the boulders and rocks of the upper valley of Wintergasse.

The route into Wintergasse is on the crest of a lateral moraine on the north side of the valley. The route always stays high on the north side, going over boulders and snow into the back of the valley. There is usually a large snowfield to cross here. It is not steep and if plenty of time is taken it can be less tiring than the interminable rocks. The way is shown by the tracks of previous parties high into the back of the valley. Near the top, turn left to an obvious cleft in the rocks of the ridge. This is Kapruner Törl.

Kapruner Törl is very narrow and the path immediately dives down steeply, tending to the right (northwest) across the mountainside. At a rock outcrop it drops down, again steeply, onto the jumble of boulders that once was Torkees glacier. The way through the blocks and boulders is marked with paint splashes, but do not expect any made-up path as you scramble and twist through the maze. Eventually, with the boulders behind, the path comes out on flat ground near a wide stream. This stream has to be crossed to its left bank wherever it looks shallow or slow-flowing enough — it may be necessary to remove boots and socks and wade across. The path is easily followed to the left away from the stream and across another steep mountainside down towards the stream that feeds the Tauernmoossee reservoir.

Just before you reach the stream, the path cuts back right to a bridge across the ravine, which the stream has carved out at about 2020 meters. Turn left once over the bridge and follow the path,

Miniature meadow tops a rock. (Tyrolean National Tourist Office, Innsbruck, photo)

sometimes boggily, up to a cairn marking a junction. Turn left again, up and across the mountainside, then under some cliffs — there are steel wires and a ladder fixed along this section — to Weissee reservoir. Go around the mountain on a track to the right and up to Rudolfs Hütte.

Rudolfs Hütte is the least hutlike hut in the Höhe Tauern; it is more of a hotel and reflects this in its prices. In 1979 it became the Alpine Center and training school for the Austrian Alpine Club and so is always busy, too organized (one has to book meals in advance, pay on arrival, and line up at a serving window for food), and is confusingly large. It does, however, have advantages like hot showers included in the price and a cable car down to the valley for easy access.

Throughout the day the views of the close glaciers around Kapruner Törl and more distant mountain ridges have been stupendous. At Rudolfs Hütte the views are just as good, stretching across the lake to Sonnblickkees and the peaks of Stubacher Sonnblick and Granatspitze, and into the wild Odenwinkel towards Johannis Berg.

DAY 3

Rudolfs Hütte (2315 m) to Kalser Tauernhaus (1755 m) via Kalser Tauern (2513 m)

Time: 3.5 hours
Distance: 10 kilometers (6.2 miles)
Viewpoints: Kalser Tauern
Access: Enzinger Boden

The path from Rudolfs Hütte to Kalser Tauernhaus is well marked and easy to follow; the only possible difficulty is snow or thick mist obscuring the paint marks on the descent from Kalser Tauern.

Go back down to the track near Weissee from Rudolfs Hütte and to the bottom station of the Medelz chair lift. Cross the small concrete bridge and take the right-hand path (711) slightly uphill. Stay to the right of the ridge up to Medelzkopf, keeping well above the lake; do not take the shore path below. The red paint markings are plentiful and lead around some rock bluffs, always getting higher, into a small valley at the head of which is the pass, Kalser Tauern.

Just as the path enters this valley, you encounter a junction with another path, the St. Poltner Ostweg, which goes off right to Granat Scharte and St. Poltner Hütte. However, continue over rocks into the valley on the right-hand side. Cut across a rock outcrop to the left and walk easily up to the pass. There may well be some snow there, even late into summer.

Kalser Tauern not only separates the west-lying Granatspitz mountain group from the Grossglockner group, but is also a pass across the main Alpine ridge from north to south.

The route down from Kalser Tauern may need careful navigation if a lot of snow is on the ground or in bad visibility. Note on the map that the path is now generally southwest down to Erdiges Eck, but it does cut backwards and forwards to find the easiest way down through the rock outcrops. Although there may have been an obvious well-trodden track through the snow on the way up, it must be remembered that Kalser Tauern is the objective of many day visitors who come up on the cable cars to Rudolfs Hütte. Any tracks in the snow on the far side of Kalser Tauern must be treated with suspicion as they could have been made by people milling about to waste time until the return to Rudolfs Hütte.

From the pass, follow the paint markings steeply down a little way and then across the mountainside to another rock outcrop. Here the path turns back right and down, then left again to the top of a prominent snout, sticking out from the general slope. The path goes to the left of this but soon regains its ridge and crosses it to the right side. It is then a simple matter to zigzag down the grassy slope to the junction of paths at Erdiges Eck.

The Selisia Hohenweg goes right at the junction, signposted to Sudetendeutsche Hütte. Keep to path 711 on the left side of the stream and head down the Dorfer Tal. The path is easily followed as it goes down to Dorfer See, becoming a little more level and rocky, only to drop down steeply again to the meadows and trees by Kalser Tauernhaus.

Map consultation provides an excuse to rest and view the scenery. (Richard Cox photo)

DAY 4

Kalser Tauernhaus (1755 m) to Studl Hütte (2801 m) via Taurer (1491 m)

Time: 6 hours
Distance: 12.5 kilometers (7.75 miles)
Viewpoints: Freiwandspitze; Studl Hütte
Access: Kals

This is a very energetic day, with a long climb up Teischnitz Tal from Taurer to Studl Hütte, but the way is easy underfoot.

From Kalser Tauernhaus head down Dorfer Tal on the track right through the magnificent large gorge of Dabaklamm to the hamlet of Taurer. The Taurer Wirt hotel, a few meters down the road, is most welcoming to walkers who require sustenance before the long haul up to Studl Hütte.

Carry on down the road from the Taurer Wirt another few meters to a parking area and junction of roads. Turn sharply left and follow this road back up into Teischnitz Tal. There is a shorter way up from Taurer to Teischnitz Tal on a path through woods, but it is awfully steep.

Teischnitz Tal runs northeast and then turns to a northerly direction. The path is on the south side of a stream and leaves the

Enjoying an alpine afternoon (Tyrolean National Tourist Office, Innsbruck, photo)

road just before a bridge. The path shown by the Alpine Club map as being on the north side of the stream does not actually exist, but luckily the correct path is also shown. This starts on a bit of a track, but after only a few twists and turns becomes a footpath going steeply through woods. It turns when it emerges from the woods.

Here is the second difference from the maps, as the way actually goes through the gorge at Mauriger Trog on a very well-made path under some cliffs and above others, instead of skirting high up the mountainside as indicated by the maps. Once through the gorge, the path turns right up the slopes and zigzags to rejoin the old path. High up on the flanks of Freiwandspitze it leads northwards and upwards towards the fantastic views of the glaciers hanging on the side of Grossglockner itself.

Studl Hütte does not come into sight until the path turns slightly right and begins to level out onto Fanatscharte, the pass on which the hut stands.

Standing on a ridge that runs directly from the summit of Grossglockner, amid glaciated mountains, Studl Hütte commands a pleasing outlook. The hut is named after Johann Studl, a German who did much in the second half of the nineteenth century to open up the Glockner region for climbing.

DAY 5

Studl Hütte (2801 m) to Glorer Hütte (2642 m)

Time: 2.5 hours
Distance: 5 kilometers (3.10 miles)
Viewpoints: Medlscharte
Access: Kals

This is a short day sandwiched between two fairly lengthy days, and will be appreciated by most parties. However, a quick group could do this day's walk together with either the previous or the next day's to cut a day out of the total itinerary.

The route to Glorer Hütte is well marked throughout and is easy to follow, but one or two places need extra care in the wet.

Go down from Studl Hütte southeast on path 702; it zigzags through the rocks and then goes down to 2550 meters, where there is a junction of paths. The main path, the right-hand one, carries on down the valley to Luckner Haus and a road to Kals. However, you must take the left-hand path on its tortuous and occasionally precipitous way to Glorer Hütte.

From the junction the path goes down slightly and around a stream bed to climb back up on the steep slopes on the east side of Kodnitztal, past a junction with another, less stable, path from Studl Hütte. It crosses a minor ridge and goes around the back of another side valley to a junction with a path that rather desperately climbs the scree to the left on its way to Salm Hütte. From here the going gets rougher underfoot as the path twists in and out over rock outcrops and uses steel wires and a ladder to get to Medlscharte. The path turns sharp left at Medlscharte and runs easily along the slope to Glorer Hütte.

Alternate routes: For walkers who want a closer acquaintance with the Grossglockner itself and who are prepared to cross glaciers, a two- to three-day loop starts at Studl Hütte and follows the route towards the Glorer Hütte as far as an eastward path to Salm Hütte. From there, continue east to Stockerscharte, then turn northwest to pass the Stausee Margaritze, Franz Josef Haus, and Hoffmanns Hütte. Turn southwest, cross the Pasterze glacier, and visit the Johann Hütte, then continue southwest back to Studl Hütte.

DAY 6

Glorer Hütte (2642 m) to Elberfelder Hütte (2346 m) via Peischlach Törl (2490 m) and Kesselkees Sattel (2926 m)

Time: 5.5 hours
Distance: 9.5 kilometers (5.89 miles)
Viewpoints: Kesselkees Sattel
Access: Kals; Lesach

The route to Elberfelder Hütte leaves Berger Törl, the pass Glorer Hütte is on, in a direction slightly west of south, across boulder fields on the flanks of Kasteneck. In fact, it contours right around to the south side of the mountain to the level, grassy pass of Peischlach Törl.

This pass is the dividing line between the Grossglockner group and the Schober group and a major crossroads of mountain paths: east to Mölltal, west to Kals, and south to Lesach Hütte, Bubenreuther Hütte, and Elberfelder Hütte.

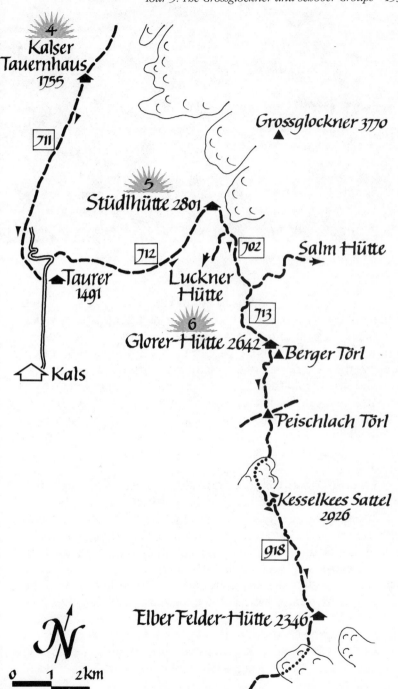

4
Kalser
Tauernhaus
1755

711

5
Stüdlhütte 2801

Grossglockner 3770

712   702   Salm Hütte

Taurer
1491

Luckner
Hütte

713

6
Glorer-Hütte 2642

Berger Törl

Kals

Peischlach Törl

Kesselkees Sattel
2926

918

Elber Felder-Hütte 2346

N

0   1   2km

Cows are both seen and heard along many alpine trails. (Bob & Ira Spring photo)

From the pass, go southeast around the left side of some high ground and onto a path on the east side of a steep stream valley, ignoring a path off to the right that goes to Lesach Hütte, Bubenreuther Hütte, and Boses Weibl. Our path, the Wiener Hohenweg, keeps to the eastern side of the main valley, first climbing up rocks near the stream and then leveling out around a flatter area where two streams meet. The way goes on around the back of the bowl but starts to climb again, over a well-made path on rocks, to a ridge coming down northwest from Gridenkar Kopf. There is a cairn on the ridge you can use as a marker if snow obscures the path markings.

From this ridge, it is possible to look southeast and see the rest of the terrain up to Kesselkees Sattel. Below and to the right is the Peischlachkessel Kees glacier, but the path stays to the left across and up a very loose, stony mountainside. The markings should be easily followed as they head up to cross the snow on the glacier just below the pass. An aluminum bivouac shelter, the Gernot-Röhr Bivouac, is on the pass. Turn around to enjoy a last view of the Grossglockner group, with its huge ice masses, before dropping down from the pass towards Elberfelder Hütte. Stay on the path instead of relying on your "sense of direction." It starts steeply on loose rocks with a cable to hang onto, but soon cuts across the mountainside in wide zigzags to the east bank of the Tramer Bach.

The path follows the bank fairly high up, then drops down and crosses the stream before the latter plunges down through rocks. Cross the water and go up on a higher mound, go under some cliffs, and head slightly downhill to a bridge across Gössnitzbach. Join the path up Gössnitztal to Elberfelder Hütte at the bridge and in a few minutes you will arrive at the hut.

DAY 7

Elberfelder Hütte (2346 m) to Lienzer Hütte (1977 m) via Gössnitzscharte (2737 m)

> *Time:* 3.5 hours
> *Distance:* 6.5 kilometers (4.03 miles)
> *Viewpoints:* Gössnitzscharte
> *Access:* Debant Tal

The only difficult section likely to be encountered today is the part of the valley below Gössnitzkees glacier, before you reach the rocks below Gössnitzscharte. This is one case where the glacier is in fact larger than shown on the maps; when you walk up this bit of the valley you are actually on the glacier. There is no danger involved in going up to the rocks if there is plenty of snow cover. However, without snow on the glacier the walk across the sloping ice is very awkward. In these circumstances, ignore the markings of the path and keep down in the bottom of the valley where there are more boulders to give a firmer footing.

From the Elberfelder, retrace the previous day's steps for a short distance to the path junction. From there, continue southwest on the south side of Gössnitzbach. The path to Gössnitzscharte goes over rocks as it climbs up to the upper reaches of Gössnitztal and is then marked through the boulders and past a right turn to Roter Knopf. It goes on fairly high but level across the lower slopes of Gössnitzkees glacier, joining the rocks just below Gössnitzscharte. Again, if you have any difficulty crossing any bare ice on this "crevasse-free" glacier, leave the path and go across the rocks and boulders lower down in the valley floor. You can then cross the mountainside away from the ice, rejoining the path as it climbs to the pass.

The path is obvious and well marked up through smoothed and scratched rocks to Gössnitzscharte. The views west from the pass show Glödis and Hochschober, two peaks of the Schober group, for the first time.

The route down from the pass continues southwest as it zigzags through the rocks, but soon turns slightly east of south along the east bank of Debant Bach as you head down Debant Tal towards Lienzer Hütte. The path drops down steadily all the way to just past the hut, then makes a sharp right through meadows to a bridge across the stream and back up to the hut.

Lienzer Hütte is pleasantly situated, not among the dramatic or oppressive scenery of high mountains and glaciers, but against the backdrop of the northerly ridge of the Schober group, among the cow meadows of Debant Tal, just above the trees and surrounded by Alpine flowers, particularly Alpenrose. There is a small emergency bivouac shelter near Gössnitzscharte. It is located north from the pass on the ridge from Gössnitz Kogel at about 2800 meters.

Alternate route: This route is also accessible from Kals to the west. To join the route from there, it is a one- or two-day walk up the Lesachtal to the Bubenreuther Hütte and over the Kalser Törl to join the route described here at the Linzer Hütte.

DAY 8

Lienzer Hütte (1977 m) to Wangenitzsee Hütte (2508 m)

Time: 2.5 hours
Distance: 5 kilometers (3.1 miles)
Viewpoints: Wangenitzsee Hütte
Access: Debant Tal

From Lienzer Hütte it is possible to go straight down Debant Tal to Lienz in about four and a half hours, but you would miss the Wangenitzsees, one of the most attractive corners of the whole Schober group.

Take the path from the hut back over the bridge and climb away from the stream, going slightly south of east. The path, the Zinkeweg, goes across the mountainside towards Untere See-

scharte (2533 meters). There are one or two steep places where the path zigzags, particularly just under the pass, but it is mostly a pleasing stroll up a grassy slope. You pass only one junction, a path to the right that goes steeply down to the valley floor. From Untere Seescharte the path drops easily down between the two lakes and around to the Wangenitzsee Hütte.

If you are interested in climbing peaks, note that Petzeck (3283 meters), the highest peak of the Schober group, can be climbed from Wangenitzsee Hütte on a marked path in two and a half hours up and one and a half hours return. It is recommended only for experienced mountain walkers but should be easy enough to navigate from map and path markings. Otherwise just enjoy the very comfortable hut and its splendid situation above the lake.

DAY 9

Wangenitzsee Hütte (2508 m) to Mörtschach (950 m)

Time: 3.5 hours

Distance: 10 kilometers (6.2 miles)

This last day takes us down Wangenitztal to the village of Mört-schach for buses back to "civilization."

The walk down Wangenitztal is straightforward. It does not take long and could be done at the end of the previous day by a party wishing to get down quickly in order to leave Mörtschach as early as possible in the morning. There are guest houses in Mörtschach.

The path from the hut leads down towards the lake, but soon swings around left under some rocks to head due east down the valley. It continues east, mostly not too steeply, crossing the stream twice to join a track at Wangenitz Alm. Follow the track as it crosses the stream yet again and keep to the lower one along the steep gorge side and around a right corner onto a paved road. A footpath sign pointing left to Mörtschach will be seen; follow the footpath down to another road that leads right and down to a bridge across the Möll River and into Mörtschach.

The bus stops on the main road just to the right of the bridge and side road you have descended on. If you have long to wait for a bus, there is a café opposite the bridge where you can sit and reflect on your magnificent walk through the Grossglockner and Schober groups. The buses from Mörtschach go north to Heiligenblut and over the Grossglockner high Alpine road to Zell-am-See, or south to Winklern and then to Lienz, Spittal-am-drau, and Mallnitz (changing at Obervellach), all of which have mainline railway stations.

—Jeremy Wilcox

TOUR 10

The Hafner, Ankogel, and Goldberg Groups

Route: *Gmünder Hütte – Kattowitzer Hütte – Osnabrücker Hütte – Hannover Haus – Hagener Hütte – Duisburger Hütte – Zittel Haus – Heiligenblut*

The Höhe Tauern, the area of high mountains and passes, contains the mighty Glockner and Venediger groups, respectively the highest and most heavily glaciated ranges in Austria. Just to the east and still in the Höhe Tauern are the less frequented but just as rugged masses of the Goldberg, Ankogel, and Hafner ranges. Further to the east, the main Alpine ridge falls away to the lower range of the Niedere Tauern, leaving Hafner as the most easterly 3000-meter peak and Ankogel as the last glaciated peak of that ridge.

The ranges are also of historical interest. Ankogel takes its place in Alpine climbing history as being the earliest glaciated peak of a fairly difficult standard to be climbed. (The modern "normal" route follows a much easier course, thanks to the position of Hannover Haus.) The first ascent of Ankogel was made in 1762, twenty-four years before the first ascent of Mont Blanc, Europe's highest peak.

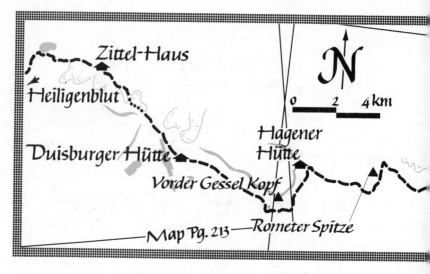

As the name implies, gold was found in the Goldberg group as early as Roman times, and even today the tourist can try his hand at panning. At its height in the mid-sixteenth century, the mining center around Kolm Saigurn was producing 10 percent of the world's gold. The industry eventually suffered from greed, in the form of excessive taxes imposed by the archbishops in Salzburg. In the area just south of Kolm Saigurn, at the head of Rauristal Valley, remnants of mine buildings may still be seen, and a museum of gold mining is located in Dollach, in the Mölltal near Heiligenblut.

There is a weather station on the top of the Rauriser (3105 meters). In 1885 the last miner at the Rauris gold mine, Ignaz Rojacher, had the idea, outrageous for the time, of constructing an observatory, to be constantly manned, on the summit. The Alpine Club took the opportunity to build a hut, Zittel Haus, adjoining the weatherman's building.

This route is at a very high level, traveling along the south side of the east-west ridge and along rough, rocky paths with the possibility of late snow patches and glacier crossings (short and easy unless otherwise stated). Several places are rendered a little safer, if not easier, by the inclusion of steel wires or bolts to hang on to. The superb views of rugged mountain scenery and the sense of achievement at having negotiated the Hohenweg ("high way" — in its literal sense) over these mountains together make a very rewarding tour.

The route starts in Maltatal near Gmund in Karnten (Carinthia) and runs east to west, crossing the spur joining the south-lying Hochalmspitze at Grosselendscharte. From the reservoir in Grosselendtal it follows the Weitwanderweg 2 (Tauern Hohenweg) to Zittel Haus on Rauriser Sonnblick, then turns down Kleines Fleisstal to the village of Heiligenblut and back to civilization.

It is possible to get to Gmund by bus from Spittal-am-Drau, which has a mainline railway station; from Gmund buses run into Maltatal. Similarly, Heiligenblut at the end of the walk is well served by public buses, to the north via Franz Josefs Höhe and the famous Glockner high Alpine road to Zell-am-See and to the south to Winklern, where buses disperse to Lienz, Mallnitz, and Spittal-am-Drau, all of which have mainline railway stations.

The paths used are well marked and, with a little care, are easy to follow. However, a few sections of the route are over rough, high terrain that can be inhospitable in bad conditions, and should be attempted only by experienced walkers and then only in good weather. A lot of these difficulties can be avoided by taking an easier route from Hagener Hütte to Sport Gastein and Naturfreundehaus Neubau (instead of to Duisburger Hütte and over Niedere Scharte) but the wild Grosselendscharte and the rock ridge to Sonnblick are the only feasible ways along the route and demand grèat care.

Huts of the German and Austrian Alpine Clubs serve the whole way well. They are at regular intervals and the distances between them are not great (rarely more than 12 kilometers). This and the fact that once over Grosselendscharte there is remarkably little variation in height along the entire route to Zittel Haus mean that the walking can be done at a leisurely pace. The huts themselves are comfortable, friendly, and reasonably priced (particularly for Alpine Club members). Only Zittel Haus has one discomfort — no water for washing — but what can one expect on top of a 3050-meter peak?

Despite the high level of the paths followed, rarely under 2400 meters, it is possible to get down to the valleys and villages quite easily, should it be necessary to buy provisions, escape the weather, or shorten the route. The recommended maps will make these "escape routes" clear, but it is easy to go to Mallnitz from both Hannover Haus (by cable car) and Hagener Hütte; to Innerfragant from Duisburger Hütte; and to Sport Gastein from Hagener Hütte. Note you must catch a bus from Sport Gastein (to Bockstein), from Kolm Saigurn (to Rauris), and from Innerfragant (to Obervellach) to find any reasonable choice of shops.

Some alpine plants are able to root in pockets of soil among the rocks. (Bob & Ira Spring photo)

The basic walk lasts seven days, but the route can be shortened by joining it from Mallnitz (thereby removing the necessity of crossing Grosselendscharte) or by leaving it on any of the escape routes.

To the east of Grossglockner, the weather is generally good, but, as in all mountainous areas, it can change suddenly and viciously. (A group I was with was once snowed in at Hannover Haus for two nights — in August!) Always be prepared for the worst and carry plenty of both warm and waterproof clothing. Snow can make parts of the route more difficult than normal, if, for instance, the snow was particularly deep the previous winter and late in melting due to a poor summer. The best times to do this walk are between the middle of July and the middle of September.

Maps: The 1:25,000 series produced by the Alpine Club, sheets 44 (Hochalmspitze – Ankogel) and 42 (Sonnblick).

DAY 1

Gmünder Hütte (1185 m) to Kattowitzer Hütte (2319 m) via Oberen Maralm (1813 m)

Time: 3 hours
Distance: 5 kilometers (3.1 miles)
Viewpoints: Kattowitzer Hütte
Access: Maltatal

A convenient bus leaves the center of Gmünd in Liesertal mid-morning, arriving at Gmünder Hütte about an hour later. This allows time for refreshment at the hut and a gentle pace up the sometimes steep zigzags on the path to Kattowitzer Hütte, which can be reached during the afternoon without raising a sweat, despite the height climbed (1135 meters). If the morning bus does not fit in with your arrival time in Gmünd, you can still take a later bus to Gmünder Hütte. This would mean not only an extra night in an Alpine Club hut, but also more time on the morrow to slog up to Kattowitzer Hütte.

From Gmünder Hütte, the path winds its way very steeply up through the trees to join a forest track at a hunting shack at 1695 meters. If you don't mind missing Gmünder Hütte, you can even take the early bus further up Maltal, about 3.5 kilometers past

Gmünder Hütte, through a series of hairpin bends and short tunnels, and ask the driver to stop at a parking area where the forest track meets the road. The track is closed to private cars. Follow this track, which is far more gentle than the path, up to the hunting shack. The forest track route saves about forty-five minutes' walking time and 328 meters of ascent.

From the hunting shack take the track on upwards to Oberen Maralm (1816 meters) and then switch to the path again (547). It follows an easier gradient through thin conifer and larch woods until a height of approximately 2000 meters is reached. Here the path zigzags steeply up to the hut, which has been in view for a depressingly long time, its blue and yellow (the town colors of Kattowitz) flag flying. The view from here is of the Hochalmspitze (3360 meters) across Maltatal and the Grosser Hafner (3076 meters) on this side of the valley.

DAY 2

Kattowitzer Hütte (2319 m) to Osnabrücker Hütte (2022 m) via Speicher Kölnbrein reservoir (1902 m)

Time: 5 hours
Distance: 13 kilometers (8.06 miles)
Viewpoints: Osnabrücker Hütte
Access: Maltatal

At Kattowitzer Hütte, turn left (northwest) outside the door and take path 545, which leads along the side of the valley gradually downwards to the dam at Kölnbreinsperre, reached in about three hours.

Although this section is overall downhill, descending 400 meters, it is fairly rough going underfoot. It starts on an open hillside, which can be muddy after rain, climbs the continuation of the southwest ridge of Hafner through a shallow pass, a rise being perceptible on the left-hand side, and soon crosses boulder fields requiring some concentration to safely negotiate — particularly if they are wet. You next reach a junction of paths. The right-hand path goes to Stickler Hütte, but you should turn left and go downhill to the flat bottom of Krumpenkar, an open space at an altitude of about 2000 meters that can get very boggy.

From Krumpenkar carry on down along the valley side on a path, now sometimes overgrown, to another junction. The left-hand way goes steeply down to the valley floor, so turn right, go uphill for a short distance, and contour along the fairly steep hillside, across a stream or two (these can be a problem after a heavy rain), to the dam at Kölnbreinsperre. You will find a modern concrete hotel at the near end of the dam. As in all places of refreshment in Austria, you are welcome to revive any flagging spirits.

The next section is the easiest of the whole route; savor it and do not be tempted to hurry along the broad easy track around the north side of the Speicher Kölnbrein reservoir. At this point you join the 502 Tauern Hohenweg. This car-size track does lead to Osnabrücker Hütte, but after leaving the end of the reservoir it is more pleasant to take the path that meanders through meadows up to the hut to the left of the track. The path leaves the track some 400 meters past the end of the reservoir.

Along the reservoir and especially from Osnabrücker Hütte looking south towards Hochalmspitze, the views are of magnificent wild mountain scenery, of rock and glacier. Osnabrücker Hütte is set in a huge amphitheater of high mountainscape, the grandeur of which will truly be appreciated on tomorrow's climb out of it.

DAY 3

Osnabrücker Hütte (2022 m) to Hannover Haus (2721 m) via Grosselendscharte (2675 m)

Time: 4.5 hours
Distance: 8 kilometers (4.96 miles)
Viewpoints: Approach to Hannover Haus
Access: Mallnitz; Seebachtal

The path to Grosselendscharte leads roughly west from Osnabrücker Hütte. Start along the track away from the hut for a few meters to where it crosses a stream (Fallbach), and turn left onto path 502 on the north side of the stream. Go up through a boulder-strewn pasture, then follow the steep zigzags at the side of a rather grand waterfall to a junction of paths on the flat area above the falls. Turn left at the junction, still on path 502. (The right-hand path goes to Zwischenelendscharte and the two lakes under Schwarzhorn.)

Path 502 continues in the same generally southwest direction across the level Fallboden and climbs, with zigzags, to the boulder field near Plessnitzkees.

Although Grosselendscharte is less than 1 kilometer away, this section of the path can be very inhospitable, an unpleasant experience in any but the best of weather. Good visibility is essential to ensure choosing the best route. After the path turns somewhat left on the boulder field, it goes down on boulders into the back of the bowl, then fairly high up until nearly under the pass, and steeply up to it. The problem is going around the back of the bowl. If plenty of snow is lingering on the glacier, it is easy to walk around on the snow to join the rocks again below the pass. There are unlikely to be crevasses on the glacier. However, if there is no snow, the route around the bowl is over the boulder jumble above the back of the glacier, and it really is a jumble, consisting of debris brought down the previous winter. There is no path and the boulders can be sharp.

If you are in doubt about the conditions at the pass, do seek the advice of the hut warden at Osnabrücker Hütte. Perhaps you can team up with a more experienced group making the same trip; if it is a fine day, someone else will probably be going to Hannover Haus.

Grosselendscharte, the high pass that separates Ankogel and Hochalmspitze, is on the ridge that divides Maltatal from Seebachtal. You can look back over the Maltatal and forward to the equally dramatic Seebachtal, which houses the village of Mallnitz, a possible escape point.

From Grosselendscharte, the path to Hannover Haus is high on the side of the valley, usually staying just below the crags and boulders on the slopes of Ankogel. It tends to wander in and out and, of course, up and down, and has an occasional cable for security.

Just after you pass the cliffs of Grauleiten Wand, there is another junction of paths. The lower, left-hand one goes to the top station of the cable car and from there climbs a steep 100 meters to Hannover Haus. The right-hand path is preferable: it loses less height and takes you more gently around, past the chapel on Arnoldhöhe, to Hannover Haus and those wonderful views of the snowy peaks of the Goldberg group in the west.

Near Hannover Haus is a cable car to Mallnitz.

DAY 4

Hannover Haus (2721 m) to Hagener Hütte (2446 m) via Mindener Hütte (2428 m)

Time: 6 hours
Distance: 13.5 kilometers (8.37 miles)
Viewpoints: Mindener Hütte
Access: Mallnitz

This route is along the Tauern Hohenweg, path 502, all the way. The path winds its way across the hillside and, although rough underfoot in places, does not lose or gain too much height.

From Hannover Haus, go steeply down to the top station of the cable car and beyond it in the same direction, down on a prominent "nose" a further 100 meters. The path cuts back sharply right and down to a junction. The left-hand path goes steeply down to Mallnitz, so take the right-hand one, which is well marked with red paint, around the back of a large basin and, generally losing height, to a pass over a rocky ridge (Luggetörl). You will pass another path to the left, again to Mallnitz, as you start to go down on boulders to a small lake (Kleiner Tauernsee). Just past the lake yet another junction of paths presents itself: right goes steeply up to a pass over the main Alpine ridge, Korntauern, also known as Hoher Tauern. Keep to the level left path, which leads over boulders and winds in and out to Mindener Hütte, reached in about three and a half hours from Hannover Haus.

Mindener Hütte is not wardened, but can be used as an overnight refuge if you have food. It offers magnificent views across Seebachtal to Maresenspitze.

From Mindener Hütte, the path continues its habit of following contour lines in and out of side stream valleys, but the terrain underfoot is a little easier. Although the hillsides are well covered with boulders, there are no more large boulder fields to cross and the path is easily followed to where it joins a track just below Hagener Hütte. There is a final short climb to the hut. (Do you wonder why the last little bit is always *up* to the hut? This is because the huts are built on small promontories to make them safe from avalanches.)

Traveling light in the high country (Tyrolean National Tourist Office, Innsbruck, photo)

At Hagener Hütte a decision has to be made on tomorrow's route. The Tauern Hohenweg continues easily to Duisburger Hütte and on over Niedere Scharte and two glaciers to Rojacher Hütte and Zittel Haus. In bad weather, the crossing of Niedere Scharte can be confusing, if not dangerous. Similarly, crossing the second glacier,

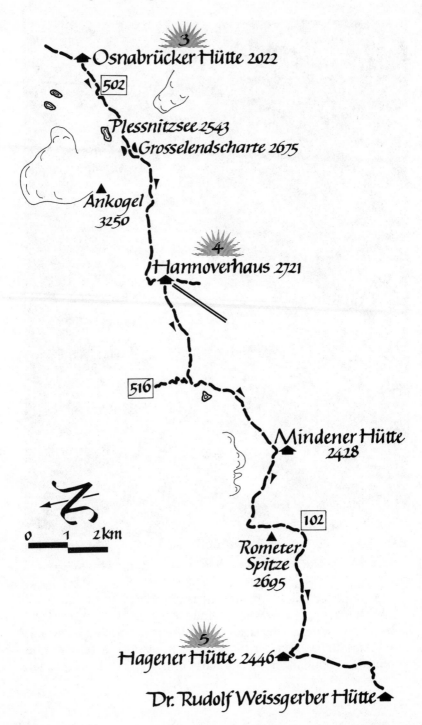

Osnabrücker Hütte 2022
502
Plessnitzsee 2543
Grosselendscharte 2675
Ankogel 3250
Hannoverhaus 2721
516
Mindener Hütte 2428
102
Rometer Spitze 2695
Hagener Hütte 2446
Dr. Rudolf Weissgerber Hütte

0 1 2 km

Ochsenkarkees, requires good visibility and good snow conditions. Even then it is advisable to use a rope, as there are crevasses. In clear weather the awkward glacier crossing can be avoided by going down on rocks to under the snout of the glacier and back up the other side again on rocks. The way is not difficult but because it is not marked, you need to be able to see clearly.

In bad weather all these difficulties can be avoided by going down northwest from Hagener Hütte to Sport Gastein and then all the way up Siglitz Tal on Herman Buhlsen Weg to Riffelscharte (2471 meters), past the burned out Niedersachsen Haus and southwest to Naturfreunde Haus Neubau (2175 meters) for overnight accommodation. This makes a long day with a lot of height variation — Sport Gastein is at 1588 meters — but it is easy walking and may be safer than crossing Niedere Scharte. It is then a simple matter to rejoin the described route on Day 6 at Rojacher Hütte by following the marked path from Neubau.

DAY 5

Hagener Hütte (2446 m) to Duisburger Hütte (2572 m) via Feldseescharte (2712 m)

Time: 5 hours
Distance: 9 kilometers (5.58 miles)
Viewpoints: Duisburger Hütte
Access: Mallnitz; Innerfragant

The way from Hagener Hütte to Duisburger Hütte is again on the Tauern Hohenweg, now path 102, and is straightforward, although it can have late snow patches.

At Hagener Hütte you leave the Ankogel group and enter the Goldberg group. The hut is at a crossroads; the one leading to your next resting place is the southwesterly Hagener Weg. It starts from behind the hut and goes slightly downhill to a junction with the path to the Vorderer Gesselkopf (2974 meters). Keep left at the junction onto a path that contours across the steep hillside on the south side of the main ridge. The going is a little "up and down" but is reasonably easy underfoot until just before Feldseescharte, where the path zigzags up on scree to the pass.

On Feldseescharte is a bivouac shelter known as Dr. Rudolf Weissgerber Hütte — a rather grand name for what is essentially emergency accommodation for six or eight people in great discomfort.

There is a path from this pass that goes southeast down to Jamning Hütte and to Mallnitz; however, turn your back to the views of Seebachtal and turn northwest into the rocky wastes of upper Fraganttal.

The path is steeply down and around a basin on the north side of a small lake, and across another boulder field that tends to have late snow patches on it. This should cause no problem if you keep a sharp lookout for red paint markings. If a snow patch is particularly steep or poses some other danger, try to climb up on the boulders and skirt around the top of the snow. Beware of snow that has melted too much to support a person's weight — this may result in slipping a leg down between hidden boulders, with the possibility of bad cuts or a twisted ankle.

Follow the path fairly high up on the rough hillside, crossing many small stream indentations until a minor ridge is reached and Duisburger Hütte and the rocky wilderness of its environs are seen for the first time, only a short distance away.

DAY 6

Duisburger Hütte (2572 m) to Zittel Haus (3105 m) via Niedere Scharte (2695 m) and Rojacher Hütte (2718 m)

Time: 5.5 hours
Distance: 6.5 kilometers (4.03 miles)
Viewpoints: Zittel Haus
Access: Kolm Saigurn

This is a day spent deep in the heart of wild high mountain country, crossing glacial debris, a glacier on steep snow, and rocks with no path markings, finally climbing a steep rocky ridge. It should not be undertaken by the inexperienced or in bad weather. If any doubts exist about conditions on the route, seek the advice of the warden at Duisburger Hütte and, if necessary, return to Hagener Hütte and take the easier and safer way mentioned at the end of Day 4.

The glaciers have retreated from the area shown on most maps, and so a lot of what appears at first to be glacier crossing is in reality a walk over loose boulders and mud, the debris left when the destructive force of the glacier recedes. Nowhere is this shown

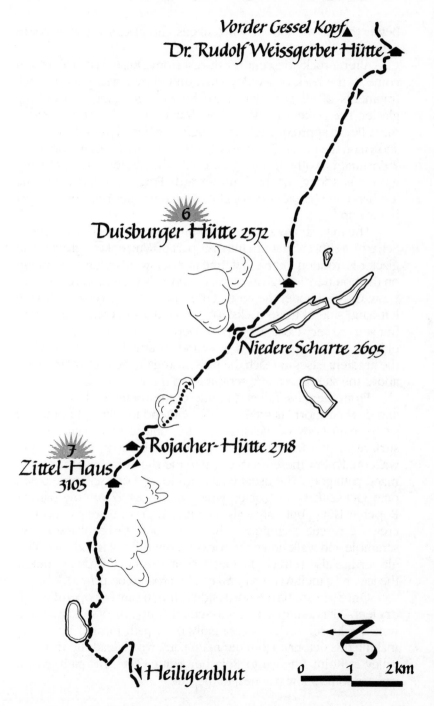

Vorder Gessel Kopf
Dr. Rudolf Weissgerber Hütte

6
Duisburger Hütte 2572

Niedere Scharte 2695

Rojacher-Hütte 2718

7
Zittel-Haus
3105

Heiligenblut

0   1   2 km

better than at the foot of Wurtenkees, the glacier below Niedere Scharte.

After a rocky descent northwest from Duisburger Hütte, you come to the back of a valley, surrounded by a wasteland of rock fragments of all sizes laid bare by the retreating Wurtenkees glacier. The route is marked, though not very well, as one goes up the valley to approximately 2525 meters, where a parting of ways is shown on the maps. Go left to what is shown as a lateral moraine at 2555 meters, without setting foot onto the glacier. The right-hand glacier is a long way back up towards Fraganterscharte and the left-hand one (as viewed from below in the valley) bothers us only higher up.

The map shows a short rock spur on the east side of Niedere Scharte, a short way south into this part of Wurtenkees glacier. The glacier is trodden for the first time just below this spur, so climb up on the boulders as high as possible and only then venture onto the snow. Go west under the nose of the spur and north close up to the left-hand side of these rocks. The snow does become steep here but you are very close to the pass. Depending on snow conditions, either continue up the steep snow and eventually move right when the gradient eases to reach the pass, or regain the rocks of the spur above the steep nose and scramble up them to the pass.

From the pass, follow the line of the route northwest across and down a short snowfield — do not tend too far right onto the steep main body of the snow — and onto a rock outcrop. The surface is firm rock this time, scratched and bared by ice but easy to walk on. Follow these rocks down to the right of where the recognized path goes. The usual path leads to a bit of a scramble down onto Ochsenkarkees glacier, which it crosses to join the path to Rojacher Hütte, but only walkers with a rope who are practiced in crevasse rescue techniques should go onto Ochsenkarkees. So scramble and walk down the rocks on the right of the glacier. This glacier has also retreated a long way; at this height you are below the ice and a melt water stream can be crossed on firm rock bed.

Once you are on the north side of the stream — hopefully with dry feet — it is a simple matter to scramble up a bit of solid rock and walk up looser rocks, occasionally on a path formed by others making this detour, to join the main path, which leads up from the valley at Kolm Saigurn to Rojacher Hütte. Take this path, which crosses some snow patches, to the hut.

Summer snow in a high alpine valley (Tyrolean National Tourist Office, Innsbruck, photo)

This whole section from Duisburger Hütte to Rojacher Hütte requires the most careful navigation and, it must be said again, should be done *only* in clear visibility.

Rojacher Hütte is a useful refreshment stop en route to Zittel Haus, but has only ten sleeping places and is a bit inconvenient to consider as a planned overnight stop.

The route from Rojacher Hütte to Zittel Haus is very popular, even as a day out from Kolm Saigurn to Zittel Haus and back, so there is no problem with route finding. Follow the red paint splashes straight up the magnificent ridge to Sonnblick. The ridge is made up of rock outcrops and blocks, and is firm if a little narrow and precipitous in places. It is not at all difficult and provides a fitting end to a most exhilarating day. The last few meters to Zittel Haus and the summit of Sonnblick (3105 meters) are accomplished on the level upper reaches of Vogelmaier Ochsenkarkees glacier.

What a view you get at the Zittel Haus: the Glockner and Schober groups tower to the west, the ridge up to Hocharn dominates to the north, and to the south and east all the Goldberg group is set out before you. If you recognize the route followed today, enjoy a bit of justified self-congratulation.

DAY 7

Zittel Haus (3105 m) to Heiligenblut (1288 m)

Time: 6 hours
Distance: 12 kilometers (7.44 miles)
Viewpoints: Zittel Haus
Access: Heiligenblut

The last day. Make the most of it by getting up early and, if you can stand the cold, watch the sunrise from the balcony around Zittel Haus. Marvel as the rosy light picks out the high peaks of the Höhe Tauern and the vistas are thrown into stark relief by the low angle of the sun. Feel the crisp morning air and the freshness of a new day. You will understand why people climb mountains, and, as the sun gets a little higher and starts to thaw the bones, why the sun was worshipped as a god.

You will need the sun to see your way clearly off Klein Fleisskees glacier, the first part of the walk down to Heiligenblut.

From Zittel Haus descend towards Goldbergerspitze for a few meters, first on rock and then on snow, until it is possible to turn right, still on snow but under the rock outcrop that supports the buildings. Follow the well-trodden track in the snow across Klein Fleisskees glacier, always fairly high up and on the right-hand side but also always descending to rejoin rocks above the Kleines Fleisstal Valley.

The path from the rocks is well used and very well marked. It crosses a ridge from Goldzeck Kopf, goes down to the lake of Zirbensee, and then easily follows the valley all the way down to the village.

—Jeremy Wilcox

TOUR 11

The Dachstein Group

Route: *Ramsau Ort – Dachstein Südwand Hütte –*
Hofpürgl Hütte – Gablonzer Hütte –
Hofpürgl Hütte – Adamek Hütte – Schilcher Haus –
Guttenberg Haus – Ramsau Ort

The Dachstein lies separate from many of the well-known mountain areas of Austria. Considerably east of the high Grossglockner region and even farther from the major mountain center of Innsbruck, it is nevertheless a walking area of great interest.

It centers on the Hoher Dachstein (2993 meters), which lies among a large expanse of glaciers and is part of a northwest/southeast ridge that is the main focus for walkers and climbers in the region.

The area lies some 50 kilometers south of Salzburg and just north of the Enns Valley, which runs like a great scar across much of central Austria. The river valley provides access points to the Dachstein, notably at Schladming, from which the walk described here rises. On the northern side of the range, the landscape slopes down towards Hallstadt on the lake which takes the town's name. The whole area is well crossed by footpaths and well provided with huts, so making this seven- to eight-day walking tour an enticing prospect.

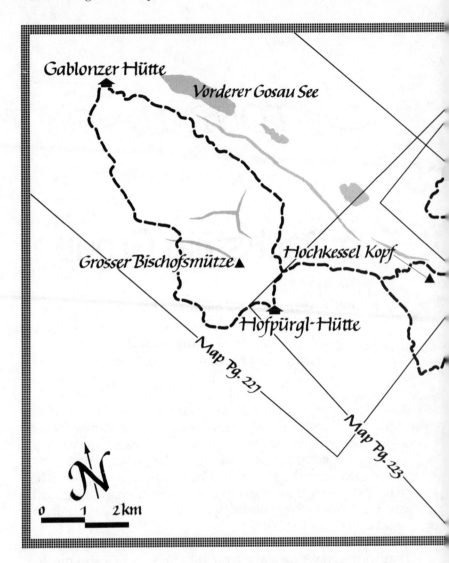

The route described here provides a fine cross section of the region, first heading northwest from Schladming, following the line of the main Dachstein massif, then crossing the ridge near the Bischofsmütze to the Gablonzer Hütte at the northwest end of the Gosaukamm. Turning almost back on itself, the route returns to the Hofpürgl Hütte, but this time along the south side of the Gosaukamm ridge before ascending that ridge to the Adamek

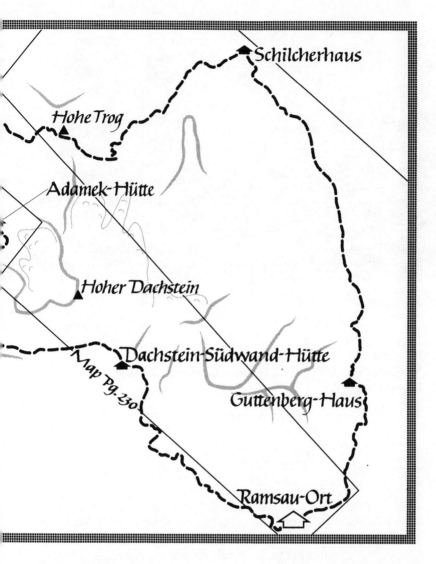

Hütte near the Grosse Gosau Gletscher. Continuing its northeasterly direction, the route crosses a small stretch of glacier to reach the Schilcher Haus before turning south to Schladming and the Enns Valley. The entire route follows marked paths and can be safely negotiated by any surefooted walker.

Maps: AV 1:25,000 No. 14, Dachstein Gruppe; Freytag and Berndt 1:100,000 No. 28, Dachstein und Salzkammergutseen

Children play against the magnificent backdrop of the south face of the Dachstein. (Austrian National Tourist Office photo)

DAY 1

Ramsau Ort (1135 m) to Dachstein Südwand Hütte (1871 m) via Austria Hütte (1630 m)

Time: 3 hours
Distance: 6 kilometers (3.72 miles)
Viewpoints: Edelbrunn; Brandriedl
Access: Schladming

A bus service connects Schladming station with Ramsau Ort, the beginning of your route. The same bus continues to the Dachstein cable lift, should you wish to shorten your first approach.

From the Ramsau Ort, go gently up past the church and school to Knoll. Follow the signs and the red and white marks that point the way to the Austria Hütte. On your way through the woods you should reach the Edelbrunn Hütte in about one hour. Refreshments and food are available there.

Now you have a choice of routes to the Austria Hütte. The lower is largely a forest track that has been graded for timber hauling. To follow this, continue past Edelbrunn and past the

A wanderer treks toward the Dachstein, the highest mountain of Styria. (Tyrolean National Tourist Office, Innsbruck, photo)

Cable car on the south side of the Dachstein massif (Leo-Heinz Hajek photo)

Dachstein Gasthof, gaining height all the way. This route takes about one hour. The higher route begins from a point just before the Edelbrunn Hütte as you approach it from Ramsau Ort. Turn right there and climb towards Brandriedl (1724 meters), a peak you can detour to before reaching the Austria Hütte. This route will take about one and a half hours.

The Austria Hütte is a favorite lunch stop for many day visitors. Although it provides accommodation, you should continue to the Dachstein Südwand Hütte to shorten the next day's walk. Continue on a well-worn path to the Türlwand Hütte, a large hotel at the bottom of the cable lift where the bus stops. On the right side of the cable station is a track that goes under the lift and around to the Dachstein Südwand Hütte, a large and comfortable stop for the night.

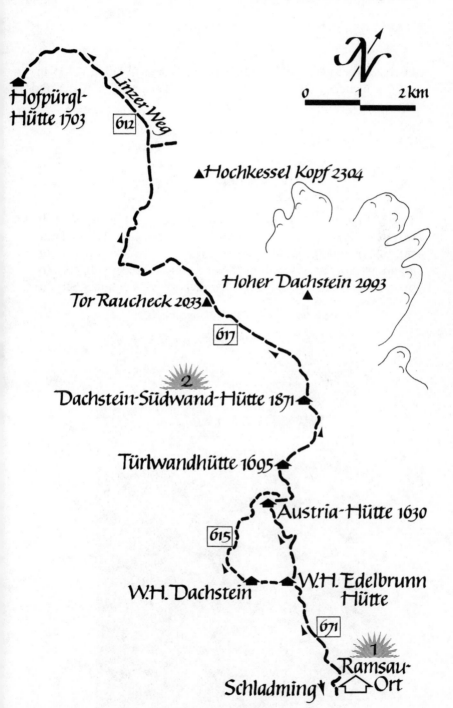

DAY 2

Dachstein Südwand Hütte (1871 m) to Hofpürgl Hütte (1703 m) via Tor Raucheck (2033 m), Windleger Scharte (2438 m) and Linzer Weg

Time: 5 hours
Distance: 11 kilometers (6.82 miles)
Viewpoints: Windleger Scharte
Access: Filzmoos

Take the Pernerweg from the Dachstein Südwand Hütte, first descending, then climbing along the south side of the Hoher Dachstein to Tor Raucheck. From here the route goes down and contours for about 1500 meters. It then passes through some scrub, crossing the track that runs north from Sulzenhals to the Windleger Scharte.

Wiesberger Haus, in the Dachstein (George Mills photo)

Join with another path running north from Sulzenhals and go gently up to a saddle (1938 meters) below the Windleger Spitze. From here, go down the zigzag path through more scrubland and on to a grassy area to contour around to the Hofpürgl Hütte. Join the Linzer Weg as you take a more westerly direction.

The Linzer Weg roughly contours along the side of the ridge, passing tomorrow's northward track to the Steiglpass and finally turning south for a short way to the Hofpürgl Hütte.

This hut offers excellent accommodations — those in the older section of the building are less expensive — and excellent *Kaiserschmarrn.* Behind the hut is the Bischofsmütze, a spectacular limestone peak not, unfortunately, recommended for walkers.

DAY 3

Hofpürgl Hütte (1703 m) to Gablonzer Hütte (1550 m) via Steigl Pass (2012 m) and Scharwand Hütte (1360 m)

Time: 4 hours
Distance: 8 kilometers (4.96 miles)
Viewpoints: Steigl Pass
Access: Road at west end of Gosau See

Days 3 and 4 are circular, returning to the Hofpürgl Hütte. The route circumnavigates the Gosaukamm ridge running north and west from the Bischofsmütze and offers spectacular views of its limestone peaks.

Start by retracing yesterday's steps for about 1.5 kilometers on the good path north to the Steigl Pass. The path is stony at first and then climbs a rock ledge, accompanied by fixed ropes. From the pass you can see the hut you have just climbed from. To the west you can see the Bischofsmütze; looking east you can see a ridge leading to the Steiglkogel, a climb of about forty-five minutes from the pass, using fixed ropes.

From the pass, the path descends gently into an area of scrubby fir trees and into a rocky limestone valley. Ahead you will be able to see the Gabelkogel (1909 meters). Pass a deep hollow known as the Eisgrube and continue along the Steiglweg, running along the northeast side of the Gosaukamm. During one open section of the walk, you will be able to see all the way to your destination, the Gablonzer Hütte. The path then runs almost level for about 3 kilometers, with peaks on the left and cliffs falling to the lake on your right.

You will pass a small chapel in memory of those who have died in the Gosaukamm, especially a woman who was killed while rappeling (abseiling) off the Daumling, a rock pinnacle which she had just earned the honor of being the first woman to climb.

Later, pass the Scharwand Hütte, a nonwardened establishment; if you plan to stay or eat here, you must take your own food and collect the key from the warden at his valley address. Check its status with the AAC beforehand.

Leaving the Scharwand Hütte, continue down, but look for the path branching to the left, which contours to link with the path from the Gosau See. Go up this for about thirty minutes to the Gablonzer Hütte. It is very popular during the daytime because of its proximity to the lift from the Gosau See, but when the valley visitors have left you will be able to enjoy the peace and quiet.

DAY 4

Gablonzer Hütte (1550 m) to Hofpürgl Hütte (1703 m) via Austria Weg and Theodore Körner Hütte (1466 m)

> *Time:* 4 hours (plus three for a round trip
> to the Grosser Donnerkogel)
> *Distance:* 8 kilometers (5 miles) plus 3 kilometers
> (1.9 miles) round trip for summit climb
> *Viewpoints:* Törleck Sattel
> *Access:* Filzmoos

Leave the hut on the Austria Weg, climbing gently for the first five minutes. You will have a good view of cliffs to your left. Climb to the Obere Törlecksattel (1594 meters) and then to the Untere Törlecksattel (1575 meters).

From the second saddle, the route to the summit of the Grosser Donnerkogel (2054 meters) branches off left. The summit offers fine views of the Gosau See and other peaks of the Gosaukamm; this detour takes about three hours round trip. If you decide to make the climb, follow the path roughly south as it traverses and rises to 1866 meters at the foot of a rock spur. Go around the spur to the left and then climb much more steeply to the

summit. On the way back to the pass, you will be able to see the Theodore Körner Hütte below and to your south.

After returning to the Untere Törlecksattel, turn left and continue down the west side of the Gosaukamm to Stuhl Alm and the nearby Theodore Körner Hütte. The hut is in a picturesque location and is available for accommodation if you are not planning to return to the Hofpürgl Hütte today. If it is full, try Stuhl Alm. Those who wish to continue climb gently, then steeply, for about two hours. You will have the Bischofsmütze straight in front of you. Pass a hunting lodge and then bear right and go steeply up a gully called the Durchgang (throughway) to a small pass, marked on the map simply as *Jöchl,* that marks the end of your views of the southwest face of the Gosaukamm and the beginning of a wider panorama to the south.

The Austria Weg continues in a southerly direction, following the contours and then gradually climbing beneath the Bischofsmütze to reach the Hofpürgl Hütte.

DAY 5

Hofpürgl Hütte (1703 m) to Adamek Hütte (2196 m) via Reissgang Scharte (1954 m)

Time: 5 hours
Distance: 8 kilometers (4.96 miles)
Viewpoints: Reissgang Scharte
Access: Gosau See

From the Hofpürgl Hütte, backtrack the final steps of Day 2 north towards the Bischofsmütze and then east along the Linzer Weg. After about 3 kilometers, fork left and climb very steeply towards the Reissgang Scharte. Some of this climb is on metal foot- and hand-holds, but it presents no great difficulty and continues up to the Hochkesseleck (2200 meters), from which you can see the Adamek Hütte.

Continue down at first, then contour around this rather bare terrain, which was left behind by the receding glaciers, and finally to the hut. Because water is hard to obtain in these limestone mountains, washing facilities are severely restricted here.

DAY 6

Adamek Hütte (2196 m) to Schilcher Haus (1739 m), via Hosswand Scharte (2197 m), Höhe Trog (2354 m) and Simony Hütte (2206 m) (2206 m)

Time: 7 hours
Distance: 12 kilometers (7.44 miles)
Viewpoints: Simony Hütte
Access: Hallstadt

Follow the route down towards the Gosau Tal, losing some 250 meters. Fork right at a signpost and go up through typical limestone landscape to the Hosswand Scharte. Head down, skirt the foot of the Hosskogel, and continue up to the Höhe Trog, the highest point of the day. From here it is another thirty minutes down to the Simony Hütte, which should take five hours to reach from the Adamek Hütte.

The route continues down the approach track for twenty minutes, then turns right and goes down through scrubby stunted trees, losing some 500 meters of height in two hours before it reaches the Schilcher Haus at Gjaid Alm. This is a privately run hut and provides excellent food, refreshments, and accommodation. Nearby lifts bring many visitors during the day.

DAY 7

Schilcher Haus (1739 m) to Guttenberg Haus (2137 m) via Feisterscharte (2193 m)

Time: 5 hours
Distance: 9 kilometers (5.58 miles)
Viewpoints: Feisterscharte
Access: Hallstadt; Schladming

Go directly from the hut towards the hotel at the end of a lift, then on a gentle path through mixed scrub, grass, and the fantastic weathered shapes of limestone rocks. There are two springs just off the path.

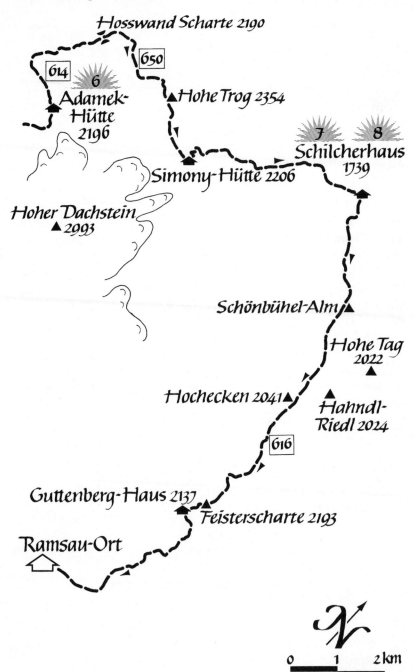

Hosswand Scharte 2190

650

614

6
Adamek-
Hütte
2196

▲Hohe Trog 2354

7   8
Schilcherhaus
1739

Simony-Hütte 2206

Hoher Dachstein
▲ 2993

Schönbühel-Alm▲

Hohe Tag
2022
▲

Hochecken 2041▲   ▲Hahndl-
Riedl 2024

616

Guttenberg-Haus 2137

▲Feisterscharte 2193

Ramsau-Ort

0   1   2 km

For about 7 kilometers there is no great change in height, until the small drop into the Hölltal. This is followed by a climb to the Feisterscharte, from which you can see the Guttenberg Haus, situated on the shelf above the valley of the River Enns, with a panoramic view of the distant Schladminger Tauern on the far side. From here it is a short descent of no more than half an hour to the Guttenberg Haus.

DAY 8

Guttenberg Haus (2137 m) to Ramsau Ort (1135 m)

Time: 2.5 hours
Distance: 4 kilometers (2.48 miles)

This section can also be walked on Day 7 by parties whose schedule demands it and whose fitness allows.

It is an easy walk down the approach route of the hut, largely on car-sized tracks, to the scattered neighborhood of Ramsau Ort. The bus can be boarded for a return to Schladming and onward travel by train and bus.

—George Mills

Glossary

Abfahrt	departure (of trains)
Abort	toilet
absteigen	to descend
Ache	river or stream
Alm	Alpine pasture
Ankunft	arrival (of trains)
Aufstieg	ascent
Auskunft	information, inquiry
Bach	stream, brook
Bahnsteig	platform (train station)
befahrbar	passable, practicable
Berg	mountain
Bergführer	mountain guide
Berggasthof	mountain inn
Bergsteiger	mountain climber
Bergsteigeressen	"mountain climber's food"; usually meat, and potatoes or pasta
Bergwanderer	mountain hiker
Blatt	map sheet
Briefmarke	postage stamp
Dorf	village
Eisenbahn	railway
Erbsensuppe	pea soup
Fels	rock
Ferner	glacier
Fernsprecher	telephone
Flughafen	airport
Frühlingsuppe	vegetable soup
Gasthaus, Gasthof	inn, hotel
Gaststube	guest room or common room (in huts)
Gebirge	mountain range
Gletscher	glacier
Gulaschsuppe	spicy, thick, stewlike soup
Haltestelle	bus stop
hoch	high
Höhe	high
Hütten Wirt	hut warden or manager
Joch	pass
Jugendherberge	youth hostel
Kaiserschmarrn	sugar-covered pancake served with stewed fruit or jam
Kamm	crest or ridge

Knödel	a big bready dumpling
Kopf	peak
kurz	short
Lager	camp
Landgrenze	boundary
Landkarte	map
Lebensmittel	provisions, foodstuffs
Leberkäse	Spam-like meat
links	left
Materialseilbahn	cable car used to transport goods from valley to hut (not for passengers)
Matratzenlager	"mattress camp," dormitory
nur für Geubte	only for experienced hikers
Pickel	ice axe
Postamt	post office
rechts	right
Regen	rain
Sattel	saddle, pass
Scharte	narrow gap or pass
Schlafraum	dormitory
Schnee	snow
schwierig	difficult
See	lake
Speisekarte	menu
Spitze	summit or peak
Stausee	reservoir or dam
Steig	steep path, climb
Steigeisen	crampons
steil	steep
Stunde	hour (often abbreviated as Std. on route signs)
Tal	valley
Tauern	pass
Teewasser	hot water for drinks
Trockenraum	drying room
Verbandzeug	bandage
von ... nach	from ... to
Wald	forest, woods
Wanderweg	footpath, trail
weit	far
weiter	farther
Wetter	weather
Zelt	tent

Index

ABOUT THE CONTRIBUTORS

GEORGE MILLS bought a train ticket to Innsbruck in 1955 without knowing anything about Austria, its language, or its people. He has been back every year since and has led Ramblers Holidays tours in the Lechtal, Stubai, Zillertal, Dachstein, and other regions of the Alps. He has prepared itineraries for Ramblers tours and has written a column on walking for *Sussex Life* magazine. He lives in Burgess Hill, Sussex, England.

BOB POORE has been on climbing and walking holidays for over twenty-five years in Britain, Austria, and Switzerland. These include an ascent of the Matterhorn. He is a member of the Austrian Alpine Club.

MARGARET STICKLAND has walked in mountains in Britain and Austria for the last twenty years. She is a member of the Austrian Alpine Club and lives in London.

BELINDA SWIFT has been visiting the Alps since she joined the Austrian Alpine Club in 1967. She has been a mountaineer since childhood and her expeditions have included ski-touring in the Ötztal and visits to Afghanistan, Northern India, Nepal, and Peru. She has published a book, *Teheran to Kathmandu,* and articles on her mountain travels have appeared in climbing club journals. Her home is near Leeds, England.

JEREMY WILCOX, a resident of Harrogate, England, has been a regular visitor to the Alps for over ten years, mainly as a leader of Ramblers Holidays groups. He has walked in the Vorarlberg, Silvretta, Ötztal, and Zillertal, although most of his Austrian Alpine experience has been in the Höhe Tauern areas of Venediger, Glockner, Goldberg, Ankogel, Schober, Lasörling, and Riesenferner. On the southern edge of the Höhe Tauern is the area of St. Jakob im Defereggental, which he describes as his "spiritual home."

Photo by David Becker

ABOUT THE AUTHOR

JONATHAN HURDLE has been an Alpine enthusiast since "discovering" the European Alps in the late 1970s. He has led hiking expeditions to the Swiss and Austrian Alps, has walked much of the Austrian range, and has tackled all walking standards included in this book. He has stayed in mountain huts of every description.

In the Swiss Alps, he led a group along the 200-mile Alpine Pass Route, which inspired him to write a guidebook by the same name, published in 1983.

His other mountain experience includes many trips in the mountains and moorlands of England, Scotland, and Wales. He is a native of London, now living and working as a journalist in New York.

Our thanks to the Tyrolean National Tourist Office in Innsbruck for the photos that they supplied for use in this book. Special thanks also to Kurt Beam, Honorary Representative of the Tyrolean Tourist Board for his assistance.